Quilts To Come Home To

Joy Hoffman & Darlene Zimmerman

Quilts To Come Home To

By Joy Hoffman & Darlene Zimmerman

Published in the United States by EZ Quilting by Wrights

Book Producer and Editor: *Eleanor Levie; Craft Services, LLC*

Book Designer: *Lisa J. Palmer*

Photographer: *John P. Hamel*

Copyeditor: *Barbara M. Webb*

Illustrator: *Mario Ferro*

Project Manager: *Pamela Callinan, EZ Quilting by Wrights*

Printed in China by Regent Publishing Services, Limited

First Edition

Library of Congress Cataloging-in-Publication Data

Hoffman, Joy & Zimmerman, Darlene
     p. c.m.
   Quilts To Come Home To
   1.Quilting—Patterns 2. Patchwork— Patterns I. Title

ISBN: 1-881588-30-0

Acknowledgments

Joy and Darlene offer heartfelt thanks to the following:

Pam Callinan at EZ Quilting by Wrights for her vision to see this book published

Eleanor Levie for making it happen with style and grace!

Our quilting friends for their encouragement and support

Fairfield for supplying batting; A&E Thread Co. for providing thread; Chanteclaire Fabrics for their fabrics

Bonnie Erickson, who machine quilted "Woven Geese"

Char Lemcke, for her machine quilting on "Big & Little Fishies" and on "In Full Bloom"

Lin Grinde, from DarLin Quilts, for her free-form quilting on "Pine Grove"

The photograph of Joy Hoffman was taken by Kevin Hoffman; the photo of Darlene Zimmerman is by Blake Stillwell of Meyer Studio, New Ulm, MN.

Photographs were taken at the Ash Mill Farm Bed & Breakfast, in Lahaska, PA, and at the home of Mr. and Mrs. Jack Ferrari.

Thanks for Erana Bumbardatore for consulting on the copyediting, and Susan L. Nichol for preparing the manuscript.

Illustrations on pages 68–71, 75, and 76 are by the design department of Wm. Wright Co.

CONTENTS

INTRODUCTION

Quilts and quiltmaking: Both give us a peaceful retreat from the stresses of life. A home warmed up with quilts provides us with visual and physical comfort, and the very process of quiltmaking can be so satisfying and rewarding.

 Quilts often bring out special emotions for the quilter as well as for the recipient of the quilt. The Yankee Doodle Stars design (pages 16, 20) certainly speaks to feelings of patriotism as well as the simple pleasure of a Fourth of July picnic. A quilting project is a wonderful way to commemorate many special family events: a "dowry" quilt for the wedding this past summer of Darlene's eldest daughter (see page 15), a pillow with photo transfers of Joy's daughter's graduation (page 9). Whatever the occasion or reason for making a quilt, perhaps for a gift, or "just because," we hope you enjoy making the projects in this book.

Many of the patterns in this book are inspired by classic designs from a time long ago, when we imagine life was less chaotic. We've added our own creative expressions to these traditional patterns, using our favorite tools to make the process easier, faster, and more fun. For example, a basic Pinwheel block was given a new spin in the Gentle Breezes quilt (see page 30) and transformed into a flower block for the quilt named In Full Bloom (page 36).

As you page through this book, we hope you will be inspired to make some of the quilts you see. Perhaps the quilt suits you exactly as we have done it—if so, the Fabric & Cutting Guides and the How-To's will make that easy and almost foolproof. You will see exactly how many strips to cut from each fabric, then which tool to use to cut the shapes you'll need. Refer to the Tool Tutorial (starting on page 68), even if you are already familiar with the tools, for clear directions on tool use. The newest

member of the tool group is the Tri-Mate™, which Joy designed as a partner to the Tri-Recs™ tools. You'll see many designs in this book that call for the Tri-Mate™ and provide a great opportunity to get acquainted with this new member of the tool family.

Everyone has tremendously varied tastes in decorating as well as in quiltmaking. In this book, we offer a different size for most of the designs. However, you may want or need something else— perhaps a Charlotte's Garden design to fit your sister's double bed, or the Pine Grove pattern used as a square wall hanging. In these cases, you'll want to add or subtract from a design to make it suit your situation. The Triangle Table on page 72 is a great reference for such pattern changes. It will tell you the number of triangles that each tool cuts across a strip of fabric. It's all listed for you, taking the guesswork out of figuring out how much fabric and how many cuts you'll need.

Though you may not want to make any changes in the size of a project, you might wish to incorporate your own personal color preferences. We certainly do. Darlene, a traditionalist, tends toward Turkey reds and indigo blues from  the turn of the century, and 1930s-era pastels. Joy is originally a California girl and loves to use bright prints and sun-washed shades. The two Come Over to My House quilts, on pages 47 and 51, reflect these different tastes. However, we do like to offer each other our opinions. In fact, one of us would usually say, "Come over to my house," and the other would drive over for a brainstorming session at the drawing board and design wall, sharing our stash of fabrics and our color ideas. Invariably, this sharing of the minds would lead to a more successful result.

Even if you quilt on your own, you can get the benefit of valuable outside opinion, especially when you begin the color selection process at your local quilt shop. We usually start there, picking what one of us thinks is the most beautiful fabric in the whole shop and adding other fabrics until just the right combination happens. An opinion from a friend, a quilt shop owner, or even a stranger can help to add a missing something.

In choosing the fabrics for Gentle Breezes, Joy loved the blue and green fabrics but needed one more piece. A friend came by, took one look, and said, "Add yellow." That yellow was a wonderful, warm complement; used judiciously in small amounts, it made the quilt sing 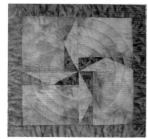 (turn to page 33 for the full effect).

Choosing a quilting design also provides an opportunity for creative and personal input. Once your quilt top is done, you'll want to consider the lines of the design and how you might want to enhance or complement them. Think about your personal preferences for swirly, free-form designs vs. neat, crisp ones; for hand-quilting vs. machine quilting; and your time frame. Is this something that needs to be done for an anniversary or christening or is it intended to stretch out over a long winter? We explain for each project how the quilting was actually done, but these are just starting points for you. Feel free to bring your own instincts to bear on this phase of quiltmaking, as for the earlier ones.

No matter whether these are quilts destined for you, for a relative, or for a friend, we hope you and your loved ones enjoy the warmth and comfort that quilts and quiltmaking bring to your lives and your homes.

Wishing you "pieceful" stitches,

Joy & Darlene

Joy Hoffman

Darlene Zimmerman

CHARLOTTE'S GARDEN

Piece a sun-splashed garden using hand-dyed fabrics in many different shades. The open space between the flowers offers a perfect place for Charlotte to add her web of quilting stitches. In a pillow of the same pattern—see page 9—each open space features a photo transfer to capture your memories.

Key Tools: Tri-Mate™, Tri-Recs™

> *Before starting either of these projects, read through the Tool Tutorial and the General Directions for Quiltmaking on pages 68–79, and the Cutting Notes as well.*

Wall Hanging

Size: 42½" square

Cutting Notes: While the table below provides yardage amounts, you may wish to consider using a collection of gradated fabrics in fat quarters for the patches. However, in order to avoid piecing the inner border, you will need yardage for those strips.

*Cut the gradated fabrics, using a good variety of shades, and arrange them in the pattern on a design wall (You may wish to include the outer flower centers, which are consistently cut from the same print fabric, for this experimental layout, too.) Refer to the photograph as a suggestion for number and placement of each shade of the color for the petals, background pieces, and inner flower centers. It's a good idea to cut more pieces from the various gradated fabrics than the chart calls for so that you can try several different layouts.

**When cutting Recs triangles, layer two strips with right sides together.

▾If you cut the border strips before you have pieced and measured the quilt center, be sure to add extra length for insurance; see page 74.

Fabric & Cutting Guide

Element/Fabric Shown	Yardage	First Cut	Second Cut
PATCHES **Petals/variegated purples***	total of 1 yard	3" strips	100 — Tri triangles
Background Pieces/ variegated greens*	total of 1½ yards	5½" strips	16 — 5½" squares 16 — 3" × 5½" rectangles
		3" strips	4 — 3" squares 40 Recs triangles** (20 pairs)
		1¾" strips	80 — Tri-Mate triangles
Inner Flower Center/ variegated yellows	total of ⅜ yard	3" strips	25 — 3" squares
Outer flower center/print	⅝ yard	5 — 1¾" strips	100 — 1¾" squares
BORDERS▾ **Inner Border/dark purple**		4 — 1½" strips	2 — 1½" × 38" 2 — 1½" × 40"
Outer Border/print		4 — 2" strips	2 — 2" × 40" 2 — 2" × 43"
BINDING/print		5 — 1¼" strips to total 180"	

How-To's

TRI-RECS UNITS (MAKE 20)

Assemble the Tri-Recs units by sewing a Recs triangle to the right side of the Tri triangle, using the "magic angle" to make alignment perfect. Press seam allowances toward the Recs triangle. Add another Recs triangle to the left side of the Tri unit. Press seam allowances toward the Recs triangle.

HOURGLASS UNITS (MAKE 40)

Sew a Tri triangle and a Tri-Mate triangle together to create half the Hourglass unit. Press seam allowances toward the Tri triangle.

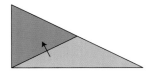

Repeat for the second half of the Hourglass shape. Stitch the two halves together, placing a pin in the seam where the points of the Tri-Mate triangles come together to help with alignment. Press the seam allowances open so that the unit lies flat.

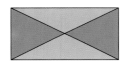

SQUARE-IN-A-SQUARE UNITS (MAKE 25)

The flower centers are Square-in-a-Square units. To make each, use 3" squares cut from various shades of yellow for the inside square—the square on point, and the 1¾" squares of print fabric for the corners of this unit. Use a ruler and marking tool to draw a diagonal line from corner to corner on the wrong side of each of the smaller squares. Place one 1¾" square in the upper right corner of the 3" square, with right sides facing, the diagonal line across the corner as shown in the diagram, and edges even. Stitch along the marked line. Trim the seam allowances to ¼"

and press them open. Repeat on the other 3 corners to complete the unit.

QUILT CENTER ASSEMBLY

Sewing & Pressing: Referring to the diagram below and photo on page 6, arrange the pieced units on a design wall. Take the opportunity to experiment with other layouts, rearranging the units to obtain a flow or balance of color that is to your liking. If necessary, sew more units to replace those you've made that don't give the effect you want. When you are satisfied with the arrangement, stitch the units together into rows; press the seam allowances in alternating directions. Then sew the rows together to complete the quilt center. Press the seam allowances toward the rows with the large background pieces.

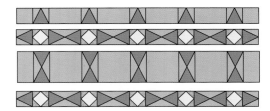

BORDERS

Referring to the General Directions for Quiltmaking, page 76, add the inner border strips, first to the sides, then to the top and bottom. Add the outer border strips in the same manner.

FINISHING SUGGESTIONS

Quilting: Mark a spider-web of concentric, curved octagons over each large, open space of the quilt top.

Layer and baste the quilt. Machine-quilt along the marked lines.

Binding: Use single-fold binding strips (1¼" wide), cut along the straight of grain. Join strips to total approximately 180", and bind the quilt, referring to page 79.

Memory Pillow

Size: 12" square with a ⅜" flange

Cutting Notes: *Do not cut out the 3½" squares until after the photo transfers have been made; see the How-To's for more information.

Fabric & Cutting Guide			
Element/Fabric Shown	**Yardage**	**First Cut**	**Second Cut**
PHOTO TRANSFERS/ white, finely-woven fabric*	⅛ yard	4 — 3½" squares	
PATCHES **Yellow**	⅛ yard	1 — 2" strip	24 Tri triangles
Light blue	⅛ yard	2 — 1¼" strips	16 Tri-Mate triangles
Medium blue	¼ yard	1 — 1¼" strip	8 Tri-Mate triangles
Yellow-and-blue print	scraps	1 — 2" strip	9 — 2" squares
BORDERS/yellow print	½ yard	2 — 1¼" × 12½" strips 2 — 1¼" × 10½" strips	
PILLOW BACK/yellow print			2 — 9½" × 12½" rectangles
FLANGE/medium blue		2 — 2¼" strips	

9

How-To's

PHOTO TRANSFERS

*Using a photo transfer paper and white fabric, transfer four 2"-square images to white fabric, aligning the edges of the photo with the fabric grain, and leaving at least 1" margin all around. Cut out the fabric so that there is a ¾" margin of white all around the photo and so that the piece measures 3½" square.

PILLOW TOP ASSEMBLY

Pieced Units: Referring to the How-To's for the Charlotte's Garden wall hanging, and using the yellow Tri triangles and the blue Tri-Mate triangles, assemble Hourglass units. For 4 units, use the same light blue fabric; for 8 units, combine a light blue and a medium blue Tri-Mate shape.

Arranging Pieces: Referring to the diagram below right, arrange the pillow top in rows; place the medium blue Tri-Mate triangles along the outside edges. Join the pieces into rows and then join the rows together; each time, press the seam allowances away from the white photo transfer squares.

Add the borders, first to the sides, then to the top and bottom. The pillow top should measure 12½" square, including seam allowances.

PILLOW ASSEMBLY

Backing: Along one 12½" edge of each of the two pillow back rectangles, make a narrow hem by turning edges ¼" to the wrong side twice and topstitching to secure. With right sides up, overlap the rectangles to form a 12½" square that has raw edges all around the sides.

Baste the opening closed. Place the pillow top, right side up, on top. Pin, then stitch all around, ¼" from the edges.

Flange Edging: Join 2¼" strips to total approximately 56". Referring to the General Directions for Quiltmaking on page 79, make and attach a double-fold binding all around the pillow, covering the raw edges and the line of stitching.

Remove the basting stitches where the pillow back pieces overlap. Insert a 12" square pillow form through the opening.

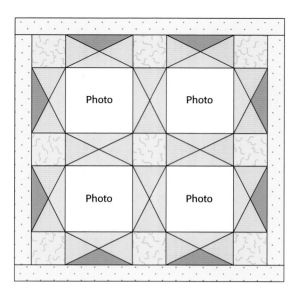

WOVEN GEESE

R ows of "geese" on the wing weave in and out as the sashing of this quilt. In a queen-size version of the design, shown above, they frame a distinctive print, appropriately quilted with feathered wreaths. A lap quilt offers an airier view of the same flight pattern; see page 15.

Key Tools: Tri-Recs™

> *Before starting either of these projects, read through the Tool Tutorial and the General Directions for Quiltmaking on pages 68–79, and the Cutting Notes as well.*

Queen-Size Quilt

Size: 80½" × 101½"

Cutting Notes: *Cut the border strips first along the length of the fabric to avoid piecing. Cut them extra-generously; trim them later to accommodate the finished quilt center. Use remaining fabric to cut some of the plain blocks; then make additional first cuts across the width of the fabric to obtain a total of 48 plain blocks each 7½" square.

▾Layer two strips right sides together to cut pairs of Recs triangles; be sure to trim off the "magic angle."

Fabric & Cutting Guide

Element/Fabric Shown	Yardage	First Cut	Second Cut
BORDERS*/mottled print	5¼ yards	2 — 7½" × 88" 2 — 7½" × 81"	
SASHING **Goose #1/brown**	1⅛ yards	9 — 4" strips	140 Tri triangles
Goose #2/blue	1⅛ yards	9 — 4" strips	143 Tri triangles
Sashing Background/cream	2½ yards	21 — 4" strips▾	566 Recs triangles (283 pairs)
PLAIN BLOCKS/mottled print		7½" strips using remaining width from borders	11 — 7½" squares
		8 — 7½" strips	37 — 7½" squares
BINDING/mottled print		2¼" bias strips to total 374"	

How To's:

Notes: This quilt is made up of plain blocks, surrounded by pieced sashing in a Flying Geese pattern: the Geese (Tri triangles) plus the background patches (Recs triangles). It is assembled in rows.

Tri Recs Units

Assemble the Geese units (Tri-Recs units) by sewing a Recs triangle to the right side of the Tri triangle, using the "magic angle" to make alignment perfect. Press seam allowances toward the Recs triangle. Add another Recs triangle to the left side of the Tri unit. Press seam allowances toward the Recs triangle.

Goose #1   Goose #2

Row A (Flying Geese Sashing; make 5)

Arrange 16 Goose #1 (brown) Tri-Recs units and 3 Goose #2 (blue) Tri-Recs units as shown in the diagram below. Repeat to make 5 rows. Label each row A.

Row B (Flying Geese Sashing; make 4)

Arrange 15 Goose #1 (brown) Tri-Recs units and 4 Goose #2 (blue) Tri-Recs units as shown in the diagram below. Repeat to make 4 rows. Label each row B.

Row C (Combination of Flying Geese Sashing and Plain Blocks; make 8)

Stitch the remaining blue Tri-Recs units together into pairs, and press seam allowances as indicated in the diagram shown at upper right.

Arrange these pairs alternating with 6 plain blocks to form a row as shown in the diagram at the bottom of the page. Repeat to make 8 rows. Label each row C.

Quilt Center Assembly

Assemble the quilt center, using the following sequence of rows: A, C, B, C. Repeat this sequence, ending with an A row.

Borders

Referring to the General Directions for Quiltmaking, page 76, add borders to the quilt top. Add the longer strips first to the sides, trimming the ends of the border strips even with the quilt top. Then add and trim the top and bottom border strips.

Finishing Suggestions

Quilting: Layer and baste the quilt. Mark an appropriately sized feathered wreath design in each plain block, and a feathered rope design along the borders. Using continuous, free-motion quilting, machine-stitch along the marked lines.

Binding: Use a double-fold bias binding (see page 79) in the same fabric as the border.

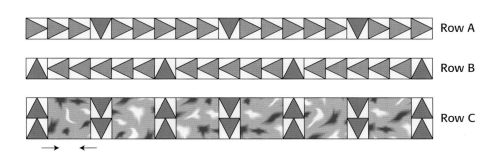

Row A

Row B

Row C

Lap Quilt

Size: 60½" × 78½"

Cutting Notes: *Cut the border strips first along the length of the fabric to avoid piecing. Cut them extra-generously; trim them later to accommodate the finished quilt center. Use the remaining width of the border fabric to cut "Geese" triangles.

▾Layer two strips right sides together to cut a pair of Recs triangles; be sure to trim off the "magic angle."

Fabric & Cutting Guide

Element/Fabric Shown	Yardage	First Cut	Second Cut
SASHING Goose #1/red	2¼ yards	8 – 3½" strips	140 Tri triangles
Goose #2/green	1½ yards	8 – 3½" strips	143 Tri triangles
Background/white	3¼ yards	18 – 3½" strips▾	566 Recs triangles (283 pairs)
Plain Blocks/white		8 – 6½" strips	48 squares
BORDERS*/red		2 – 2½" × 75½" 2 – 2½" × 61½"	
BINDING/green		2¼" bias strips to total 290"	

How-To's

QUILT TOP ASSEMBLY

Follow the How-To's for the queen-size quilt, substituting red for each Goose #1, and green for Goose #2; use the same fabric for the background pieces of the Flying Geese sashing and for the plain blocks. The sequence of A, B, and C rows is identical in this project, but refer to the photo on page 15 to check your placement of colors. As with the queen-size quilt, add the borders first to the sides, then to the top and bottom.

FINISHING SUGGESTIONS

Quilting: Use free-motion quilting with an all-over meander stitch in the background areas of both the plain blocks and the background patches of Flying Geese sashing.

Binding: Use a double-fold bias binding (see page 79) in green.

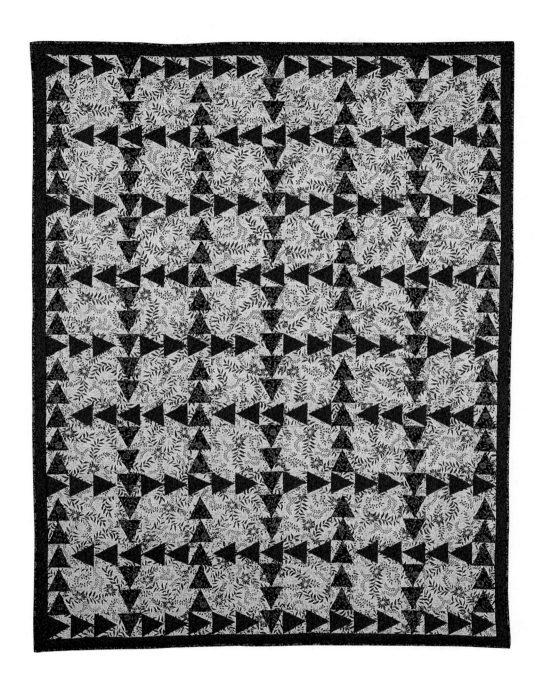

YANKEE DOODLE STARS

Hooray for the red, white, and blue! Show your true colors in a generously sized lap quilt, in which five graduated shades of blue parade behind red and white stars. For a patriotic room accent that you can make in double-quick time, try the table runner shown on pages 20 and 22. Of course, these interlocked stars would make a dazzling display in any color palette that reflects your spirit.

Key Tool: Recs™

Before starting either of these projects, read through the Tool Tutorial and the General Directions for Quiltmaking on pages 68–79, and the Cutting Notes as well.

Lap Quilt

Size: 58" × 70"

Cutting Notes: Blue fabrics are gradated from the darkest (#1) to the lightest (#5).

   *For all Recs triangles: Open the fabric strips, layer either the red or the white strips on top of the blue strips, *right sides up,* then cut. The following combinations are needed:

178 divided rectangles of red and white
22 divided rectangles of darkest blue and white
18 divided rectangles of darkest blue and red

178   22   18

Fabric & Cutting Guide

Element/Fabric Shown	Yardage	First Cut	Second Cut
PATCHES			
Background Squares/darkest blue #1	1⅝ yard	7 — 4½" strips	40 — 4½" squares
Triangles Along the Edges/darkest blue #1			40 — 4½" Recs triangles*
Background Squares/blue #2	⅝ yard	4 — 4½" strips	32 — 4½" squares
Background Squares/blue #3	½ yard	3 — 4½" strips	24 — 4½" squares
Background Squares/blue #4	½ yard	3 — 4½" strips	20 — 4½" squares
Background Squares/blue #5	¼ yard	1 — 4½" strip	4 — 4½" squares
Star Points/white	1½ yards	9 — 4 ½" strips	200 Recs triangles*
Star Centers/white		4 — 2½" strips	50 — 2½" squares
Star Points/red	1½ yards	9 — 4½" strips	196 Recs triangles*
Star Centers/red		4 — 2½" strips	49 — 2½" squares
BINDING/darkest blue		2¼" bias strips to total 266"	

How-To's

Note: This quilt is assembled in rows, rather than blocks. If possible, arrange pieces and rows on a design wall, so that the placement of pieces can be maintained as the stitching progresses.

STAR POINT UNITS

Begin by stitching together the divided rectangles of the various color combinations. Take the top unit off each pair, turn it over, and position the pieces with right sides facing; use the "magic angle" on the tips of the Recs triangles to align the pieces for sewing. Stitch together the divided rectangles of the various color combinations. Press the seam allowances toward the darker fabric.

178   22   18

NARROW ROWS OF STAR POINTS AND STAR CENTERS

A Rows: Referring to the diagram below, arrange the divided rectangles (horizontal Star points) and small squares (Star centers) in a row. Stitch the row together, and press the seam allowances toward the small squares. Repeat to obtain 6 rows.

B Rows: Referring to the diagram below, arrange the divided rectangles (horizontal Star points), and small squares (Star centers) in a row. Stitch the row together, and press the seam allowances toward the small squares. Repeat to obtain 5 rows.

WIDE ROWS OF BACKGROUND SQUARES AND VERTICAL STAR POINTS

Arrangement: Working on a design wall or large surface, arrange the A rows and the B rows, leaving a 4½" space at the top, at the bottom, and in between each row. Arrange the remaining squares (background squares) and divided rectangles (vertical Star points) to form wide rows that fill in the spaces above, below, and between A and B rows. Refer to the photograph, with its rows numbered along the right, and to the directions below for the order of the blue fabric background squares in each wide row. Rotate the divided rectangles as necessary to produce the interlocked star pattern.

Notice that the arrangement is symmetrical, top to bottom and left to right, so you can arrange the pieces in an established style. It may be easiest to start by placing the darkest blue squares along the perimeter of the quilt, and the lightest blue squares in the center.

Wide Rows 1 & 23: 10 blue #1

Wide Rows 3 & 21: 1 blue #1, 8 blue #2, 1 blue #1

Wide Rows 5 & 19: 1 blue #1, 1 blue #2, 6 blue #3, 1 blue #2, 1 blue #1

Wide Rows 7, 9, 15, & 17: 1 blue #1, 1 blue #2, 1 blue #3, 4 blue #4, 1 blue #3, 1 blue #2, 1 blue #1

Wide Rows 11 & 13: 1 blue #1, 1 blue #2, 1 blue #3, 1 blue #4, 2 blue #5, 1 blue #4, 1 blue #3, 1 blue #2, 1 blue #1

Stitching: When your arrangement is complete, stitch the pieces together in each of the wider rows. Press seam allowances toward the background squares. Replace each row, as it is finished, in the arrangement.

Quilt Assembly: Stitch the entire quilt top together as it is arranged. Press the seam allowances downward.

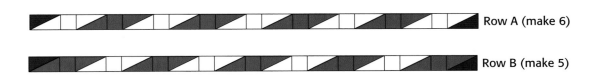

Row A (make 6)

Row B (make 5)

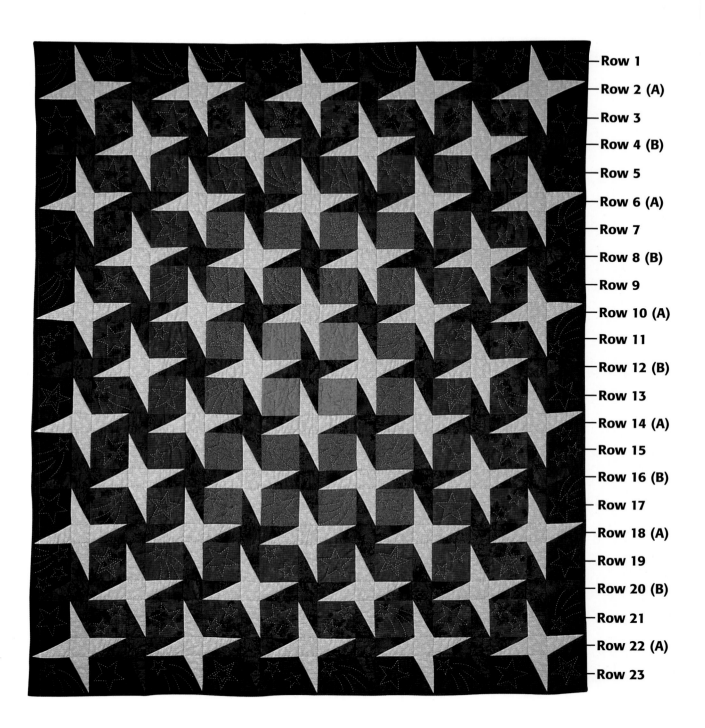

Row 1
Row 2 (A)
Row 3
Row 4 (B)
Row 5
Row 6 (A)
Row 7
Row 8 (B)
Row 9
Row 10 (A)
Row 11
Row 12 (B)
Row 13
Row 14 (A)
Row 15
Row 16 (B)
Row 17
Row 18 (A)
Row 19
Row 20 (B)
Row 21
Row 22 (A)
Row 23

FINISHING SUGGESTIONS

Quilting: Stitch-in-the-ditch around each of the white stars. To duplicate the quilting design shown, mark motifs in the center of each of the background squares, using various parts of Sliding Stencil # 8827016—*Shooting Star* (see page 80). Hand-quilt along the marked motifs, using pearl cotton #8 in gray.

Binding: Use a double-fold bias binding cut from darkest blue #1.

Yankee Doodle Stars Table Runner

Size: 23" × 41"

Cutting Notes: *Unfold each strip before cutting, and layer the two different color strips both right-side up for cutting. The following combinations are needed:

    32 divided rectangles of red and blue
    12 divided rectangles of blue and flag print
        (shown here as cream-colored)
    8 divided rectangles of red and flag print*

    32   12   8

Fabric & Cutting Guide

Element/Fabric Shown	Yardage	First Cut	Second Cut
PATCHES **Background/flag print**	½ yard	4 — 3½" strips	32 — 3½" squares 20 Recs triangles*
Star Point/red	½ yard	2 — 3½" strips	40 Recs triangles*
Star Center/red		1 — 2" strip	10 — 2" squares
Star Point/blue	⅜ yard	2 — 3½" strips	44 Recs triangles*
Star Centers/blue		1 — 2" strip	11 — 2" squares
BORDERS **Inner Border/red**		2 — 1½" strips	2 — 1½" × 17" 2 — 1½" × 37½"
Outer Border/blue		2 — 2½" strips	2 — 2½" × 19" 2 — 2½" × 41½"
BINDING/red		4 — 1¼" strips to total 138"	

How-To's

STAR POINT UNITS

Begin by stitching together the divided rectangles of the various color combinations. Take the top unit off each pair, and position the pieces with right sides facing; use the "magic angle" on the tips of the Recs triangles to align the pieces for sewing. Stitch together the divided rectangles of the various color combinations. Press the seam allowances toward the darker fabric.

Note: The background fabric, a flag print in the photographed table runner, is shown in these diagrams as a solid cream color.

NARROW ROWS OF STAR POINTS AND STAR CENTERS

A Rows: Referring to the diagram below, arrange the divided rectangles (horizontal Star points) and small squares (Star centers) in a row. Stitch the row together, and press the seam allowances toward the small squares. Repeat to obtain 4 rows.

Row A
(make 4)

B Rows: Referring to the diagram below, arrange the divided rectangles (horizontal Star points) and small squares (Star centers) in a row. Stitch the row together, and press the seam allowances toward the small squares. Repeat to obtain 3 rows.

Row B
(make 3)

WIDE ROWS OF BACKGROUND SQUARES AND VERTICAL STAR POINTS

Arrangement: Working on a design wall or large surface, arrange the A rows and the B rows, leaving a 3½" space at the top, at the bottom, and in between each row. Arrange the remaining squares (background squares) and divided rectangles (vertical Star points) to form wide rows that fill in the spaces above, below, and between A and B rows. Refer to the photograph on page 22, with its rows numbered along the right. For the top and bottom rows, combine 4 background squares, with a blue and flag print divided rectangle, then a red and flag print divided rectangle, then a blue and flag print divided rectangle, in that order, between the squares. For all other wide rows, combine 4 background squares, with a red and blue divided rectangle between each one. Rotate the divided rectangles as necessary to produce the interlocked star pattern.

Stitching: When your arrangement is complete, stitch the pieces together in each of the wider rows. Press seam allowances toward the background squares. Replace each row, as it is finished, in the arrangement.

Quilt Center Assembly: Stitch the entire quilt top together as it is arranged. Press the seam allowances downward.

BORDERS

When the center of the quilt is completed, add the narrow red inner border, first to the top and bottom rows (short ends of the table runner), then to the sides. Repeat with the wider, blue, outer border.

FINISHING SUGGESTIONS

Quilting: Stitch-in-the-ditch around each of the stars and on both sides of the inner border.

Binding: Bind, using a single fold, straight-of-grain binding cut from the red fabric; refer to page 79.

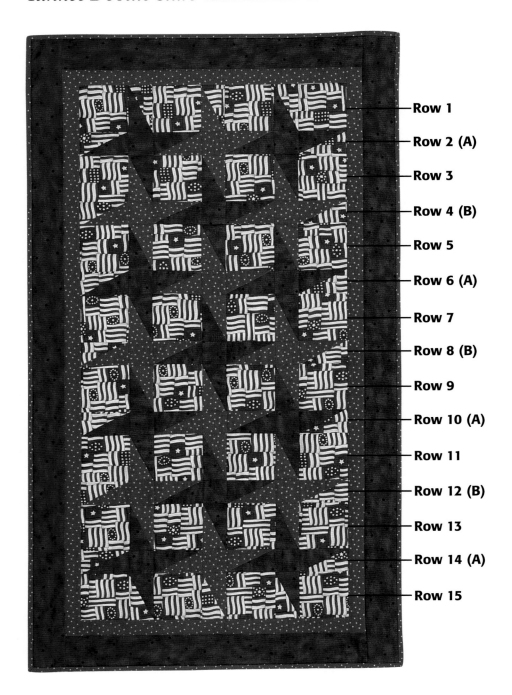

Row 1

Row 2 (A)

Row 3

Row 4 (B)

Row 5

Row 6 (A)

Row 7

Row 8 (B)

Row 9

Row 10 (A)

Row 11

Row 12 (B)

Row 13

Row 14 (A)

Row 15

BIG & LITTLE FISHIES

Dive into a whimsical, creative project: a large quilt just teeming with fish in different sizes and colors. While this design may seem complex, it's surprisingly simple, and you'll find that the cutting and piecing go absolutely swimmingly. A growth chart (see page 29) requires just four pieced blocks, so it's as much fun to make as it is to measure the increasing heights of a child through the years. With either design, there will be no need to fish for compliments on your quiltmaking!

Key Tools: Recs™, Easy Angle™

> *Before starting either of these projects,
> read through the Tool Tutorial
> and the General Directions
> for Quiltmaking on pages 68–79, and
> the Cutting Notes as well.*

Bed Quilt

Size: 78" × 90" (to fit a twin or full-size bed)

Cutting Notes: *First cut the border strips of the Blue/water fabric along the length of the fabric to avoid piecing. Cut them extra-generously; trim them later to accommodate the finished quilt center.

Use the remaining fabric to cut some of the smaller pieces needed.
▾These pieces are cut crosswise.

Fabric & Cutting Guide

Element/Fabric Shown	Yardage	First Cut	Second Cut
8" FISH Water/blue	7 yards	5 — 4½" strips	24 — 4½" squares 48 Recs triangles (24 pairs)
		6 — 2½" strips	48 — 2½" × 4½" rectangles
Fish/*each* of 3 prints	1⅛ yards each	2 — 4½" strips	16 Recs triangles (8 pairs) 16 Easy Angle triangles
		1 — 2½" strip	16 — 2½" squares
6" FISH Water/blue		4 — 3½" strips	24 — 3½" squares 48 Recs triangles (24 pairs)
		4 — 2" strips	48 — 2" × 3½" rectangles
Fish/*each* of 3 prints		2 — 3½" strips	16 Recs triangles (8 pairs) 16 Easy Angle triangles
		1 — 2" strip	16 — 2" squares
Sashing Strips/blue		10 — 2½" strips	24 — 2½" × 8½" rectangles 24 — 2½" × 6½" rectangles
4" FISH Water/blue		6 — 2½" strips	48 — 2½" squares 96 Recs triangles (48 pairs)
		6 — 1½" strips	96 — 1½" × 2½" rectangles
Fish/*each* of 3 prints		3 — 2½" strips	32 Recs triangles (16 pairs) 32 Easy Angle triangles
		2 — 1½" strips	32 — 1½" squares
Four-Patch Squares/blue		6 — 4½" strips	48 — 4½" squares

(continued)

Fabric & Cutting Guide *(continued)*

Element/Fabric Shown	Yardage	First Cut	Second Cut
SETTING TRIANGLES **Water/blue**		2 — 13" strips	6 — 13" squares, cut twice on the diagonal to yield 24 setting triangles
		1 — 8" strip	2 — 8" squares, cut once on the diagonal to yield 4 corner triangles
BORDERS **Inner Border/*each* of 3 fish prints**		3 — 1½" strips▾	2 — 1½" × 68¼" 2 — 1½" × 81½"
Outer Border/blue*			2 — 5" × 70¼" 2 — 5" × 90½"
BINDING/fish print		2¼" bias strips to total 346"	

How-To's

FISH BLOCKS (8" FISH, MAKE 24; 6" FISH, MAKE 24; 4" FISH, MAKE 48)

Note: All the fish blocks are constructed the same, regardless of what size you are making, or what direction the fish will be turned.

Tail Fins: Stitch together the Recs triangles in pairs, using one fish print triangle and one blue water triangle. Half will be "lefties" and half will be "righties." Press the seam allowances toward the fish print fabric.

Top & Bottom Fins: For each, use a small square in the same fish print fabric as used for the tail fins. Mark a diagonal line on the wrong side of this square, and layer it on a water rectangle, with right sides facing, bottom edges even, and the marked diagonal going from upper left to lower right corners. Stitch along the marked diagonal line. Make a second unit, positioning and stitching the diagonal from lower left to upper right. Refer to the diagrams under "Block Assembly" for these mirror images. Trim the excess fabric beyond the seams, leaving only ¼" seam allowances. Press the seam allowances toward the water fabric to create opposing seams.

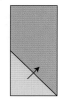

Block Assembly: Join a tail fin and a top or bottom fin, referring to the diagrams below. Press the seam allowances open.

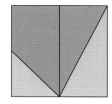
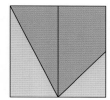

Pair two Easy Angle triangles, one for the fish head using the same print fabric as for the fins, and the other a second print, for the fish body. Stitch together to form a triangle square; press the seam allowances toward the darker fabric.

Arrange the units, plus a square of the water fabric, to form a Four Patch. Stitch the two units of each horizontal row together, and press as indicated in the diagram. Then stitch the two rows together, and press the seam allowances towards the fish head and body.

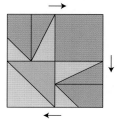

Turn the block on point, so the fish swims toward the left or the right.

8" Fish: Use the block as is, which should measure 8½" square, including seam allowances. Make 24.

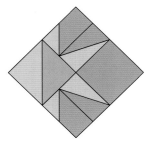

6" Fish: Add sashing strips on any two adjacent sides. *Note:* Vary the positions of these two adjacent sashing strips from block to block, to provide different spacing options for the arrangement of blocks in the finished quilt top. Press the seam allowances toward the sashing strips. The finished block should measure 8½" square, including seam allowances. Make 24.

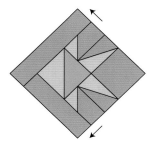

4" Fish: Arrange two 4½" fish blocks (this includes seam allowances) and two 4½" water squares to make a Four-Patch as shown, or in a different configuration. Stitch the pieces together in rows, and press the seam allowances toward the water squares. Then stitch the rows together and press the seam allowances to one side. The finished block should measure 8½" square, including seam allowances. Make 24.

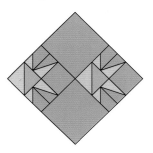

Quilt Center Assembly

Work on a design wall or a large, flat surface. Arrange the blocks on point, varying the sizes and directions of the fish. Refer to the photo for a suggested arrangement suitable for use on a bed.

Arrange the setting triangles along the edges and then add the corner triangles. (These pieces are slightly larger than needed.) Stitch the blocks and setting triangles together in diagonal rows, and press the seam allowances in alternating directions. Replace each strip on the design wall or work surface to maintain the arrangement. Stitch the rows together, and press all the seam allowances in the same direction.

Trim the edges of the quilt center evenly, being careful to leave ¼" seam allowances all around the edges. It is helpful to mark the cutting line with a chalk marker first to be sure that there are no surprises (such as blocks out of alignment) before cutting. Then, you can make minor adjustments to the line in order to keep the quilt as square and even as possible.

Borders

Inner Pieced Border: Cut each of the 1½" fish print border strips into 10" lengths. Assemble the 10" lengths alternating colors, joining with diagonal seams; press the seam allowances open.

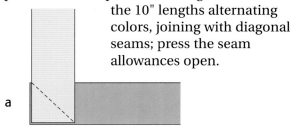

a

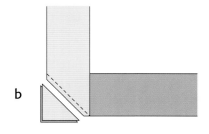

b

c

Stitch a pieced strip to the top of the quilt center, trimming the strip to fit. Repeat at the bottom of the quilt center, and press seam allowances toward the pieced borders. Stitch pieced strips to the sides of the quilt center in the same way.

Outer Plain Border: Referring to the General Directions for Quiltmaking, page 76, add borders to the quilt top. Add the longer strips first to the sides, trimming the ends of the border strips even with the quilt top. Then add and trim the top and bottom border strips.

FINISHING SUGGESTIONS

Quilting: Mark scalloped waves on the blue water fabric. Layer and baste the quilt. Stitch-in-the-ditch around each of the fish and between their heads and bodies, then quilt the marked waves.

Binding: Use double-fold bias binding; refer to page 79.

Embellishing: Add an eye to each fish, just above the center of the head, using buttons or beads (6mm and 8mm beads are used here). Alternatively, use satin-stitch embroidery to create an eye for each fish.

Growth Chart

Size: 9" × 48"

Key Tools: Tri-Recs™, Easy Angle™

How To's

FISH BLOCK (MAKE 4)

Assemble four 3" fish blocks, using the pieces indicated in the cutting chart. Refer to the bed quilt how-to's, but use the yellow print for all the fish bodies, and the multicolor print for the head and fins of each fish. If possible, choose the same color area of the multicolor print fabric for the pieces of each fish.

Sew a setting triangle on each side of each fish block. Press seam allowances toward the setting triangles. Trim and square up each block; it should measure 4¾" square.

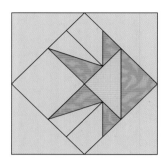

Fabric & Cutting Guide

Element/Fabric Shown	Yardage	First Cut	Second Cut
FISH BLOCKS			
Fins/multicolor print	½ yard	1 – 2" strip	8 Recs triangles (4 pairs) 8 – 1¼" squares
Head/multicolor print		1 – 2" strip	4 Easy Angle triangles
Body/yellow	scraps	1 – 2" strip	4 Easy Angle triangles
Water/aqua	⅝ yard	1 – 2" strip	4 – 2" squares 8 Recs triangles (4 pairs) 8 – 1¼" × 2" rectangles
Spacers/aqua		1 – 2¼" strip	4 – 2¼" × 4¾" rectangles
Setting Squares/aqua		1 – 3¼" strip	16 Easy Angle triangles
BACKGROUND/aqua		1 – 6½" strip	6½" × 21" rectangle 6½" × 11" rectangle
INNER BAR/multicolor print		2 – 2" strips	2" × 48½"
OUTER BAR/aqua		2 – 1¾" strips	1¾" × 48½"
BINDING/multicolor print		4 – 1¼" strips	

Panel Assembly

Arrange the fish so they all face right. Sew a 2¼" × 4¾" spacer rectangle of water fabric to the right side of three of the fish blocks, and to the left side of the fourth one. Press the seam allowances toward the spacer.

Arrange the fish units in a vertical row, placing the one with the spacer on the left second from the top. Insert the 6½" × 21" water rectangle between the third and fourth fish units. Below the fourth fish, place the 6½" × 11" rectangle of water fabric. Stitch the pieces together. Press the seam allowances toward the unpieced section where possible, or press the seam allowances between pieced blocks open, so the panel lies flat. At this point the pieced panel should measure approximately 6½" × 48".

Piece the 2" strips of multicolor print to make a strip the same length as the pieced panel. Sew to the right side of the fish/rectangle unit. Press the seam allowances toward the multicolor print strip.

Piece the 1¾" strips of water fabric to make a strip 48½" long. Sew to the right side of the multicolor print strip to complete the panel. Press the seam allowances open.

Center a yellow, 60" tape measure over the seam between the blue and multicolor strips. Place the 60" end at the top of the panel. If the tape measure is vinyl, use masking tape to temporarily hold it in place, to avoid the holes that would be left by pins. Topstitch on both sides of the measuring tape, using a thread to match the tape measure. Cut the part of the tape measure that extends past the bottom of the pieced panel.

Finishing Suggestions

Quilting: Stitch-in-the-ditch around each fish and on both sides of the tape measure. Using free-motion quilting and metallic thread, stitch scalloped waves along the water fabric, working around the fish.

Binding: Use a single-fold, straight-of-grain binding cut from multicolor print strips; refer to page 79.

Embellishing: Sew on 6mm beads to add an eye to each fish, positioning the eye just above the center of the head.

Hanging the Growth Chart: Sew sleeves to the top and bottom of the panel, and insert a dowel or wood slat through each. Alternatively, use Velcro hook-and-loop tape at the top and bottom of the grow chart: Stitch the soft loop tape to the backing of the panel, and adhere the corresponding hook tape directly to the wall or to wood slats to be hung on the wall.

Measure up the wall to position the growth chart based on where the tape measure has been cut off.

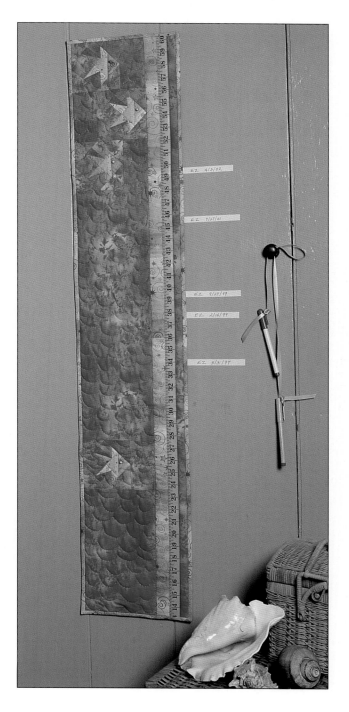

GENTLE BREEZES

This quilt, a fresh take on the classic Pinwheel pattern, will give you the distinct impression you're dozing outdoors on a lovely afternoon. Whether you make a generously sized lap quilt or the same design in a smaller-scale for a crib quilt (see page 35), the cutting and piecing really are a breeze.

Key Tools: Tri-Recs™, Tri-Mate™

> *Before starting either of these projects,*
> *read through the Tool Tutorial*
> *and the General Directions*
> *for Quiltmaking on pages 68–79, and*
> *the Cutting Notes as well.*

Lap Quilt

Size: 57" × 75"; block: 15" square

Cutting Notes: *Cut the spacer border strips *first* along the length-wise grain of the fabric. Dimensions given here are the mathematical ideal; cut these pieces extra generously, both in *width* and in *length*, and trim them later to accommodate the finished quilt center and the pieced borders (see page 76). Cut out the sashing strips from the floral print fabric that remains.

**Layer the blue and green strips, right sides together with the green fabric on top, and cut the Recs triangles. The blue and green fabrics will be in the correct position.

Fabric & Cutting Guide

Element/Fabric Shown	Yardage	First Cut	Second Cut
PINWHEEL BLOCK **Blades/ yellow print**	1 yard	6– 2" strips	48 Tri-Mate triangles
Inner Blade/blue print	1¾ yards	2 – 3½" strips**	48 Recs triangles
Outer Blade/green print	1⅛ yard	2 – 3½" strips**	48 Recs triangles
Background/mottled print	1¼ yards	6 – 5" strips	48 – 5" × 6½" rectangles
Framing Strip/blue print		10 – 2" strips	12 – 2" × 12½" 12 – 2" × 15½"
Framing Strip/green print		10 – 2" strips	12 – 2" × 12½" 12 – 2" × 15½"
SASHING/floral print*			17 – 2" × 15½" rectangles 6 – 2" squares

(continued)

Fabric & Cutting Guide *(continued)*

Element/Fabric	Yardage	First Cut	Second Cut
BORDERS Spacer Borders*/floral print	2 yards		2 — 4¼" × 65" 2 — 3½" × 56"
Pieced Borders Blue print		2 — 3½" strips	42 Recs triangles
Green print		2 — 3½" strips	42 Recs triangles
Yellow print		6 — 2" strips	42 Tri-Mate triangles
Cornerstones/yellow print		2" strip	4 — 2" squares
BINDING/blue print		2¼" bias strips to total 275"	

How-To's

PINWHEEL BLOCK (MAKE 12)

Pinwheel Blade: Sew a blue Recs triangle to the left side of a yellow Tri-Mate triangle, using the cut-off tips to make alignment perfect. Press seam allowances toward the Recs triangle. Complete the unit by adding a green Recs triangle to the right side of the Tri-Mate triangle. Press seam allowances toward the Recs triangle. Repeat to make 48 pieced triangle units.

Background: Add the background rectangle (mottled print) to each of the 48 pieced triangle units. Press seam allowances toward the background rectangles.

Block Assembly: Sew two units together to form half of the Pinwheel block. Press seam allowances as shown in the diagram (above right).

Join the halves to complete the Pinwheel block, and press the seam allowances open so the block lies flat.

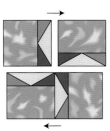

Framing Strips: Add a short blue framing strip to the left side of the Pinwheel block. Next, add a short green framing strip to the right side of the block. Press the seam allowances toward the framing strips. Add a long blue framing strip to the top edge of the block and a long green framing strip to the bottom edge of the block, pressing the seam allowances toward the framing strips.

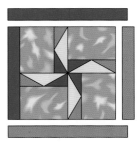

QUILT CENTER ASSEMBLY

Arrange the blocks in four rows of three blocks in each row. Add a sashing strip (as shown, a floral print) between the blocks in each row. Join the pieces within each row, and press the seam allowances toward the sashing strips.

Assemble 3 horizontal sashing strips from three 2" × 15½" sashing strips and two 2" sashing squares. Press the seam allowances toward the long sashing strips.

Join the block rows and the horizontal sashing rows. Press the seam allowances toward the sashing strip rows.

BORDERS

Pieced Border: Using the remaining 42 Tri-Mate and Recs triangles, join units for the pieced borders in the same way as for the Pinwheel blades. Sew 9 triangle units together for the top and bottom borders. Sew 12 triangle units together for each side border.

Sew a yellow cornerstone to the ends of the shorter pieced borders after you attach the spacer borders.

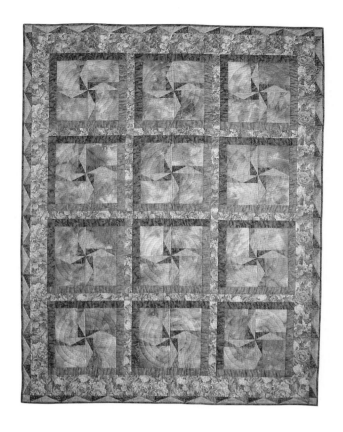

Assembly: Referring to the General Directions for Spacer Borders on page 76, measure to determine the necessary sizes and cut or trim the spacer border strips (as shown, floral print fabric) to size, so that they will span the distance between the quilt center and the pieced borders.

Stitch the longer spacer border strips (as shown, floral print fabric) to the sides of the quilt center, then stitch the shorter spacer border strips to the top and bottom. Press the seam allowances toward the spacer borders. Add the pieced border strips to the quilt in the same way.

FINISHING SUGGESTIONS

Quilting: Before layering the quilt, mark on the quilt top a design of concentric circles in each block. Use a compass set for a radius of 1", 2", 3", 4", and 5" to draw these circles. After layering, use machine quilting to stitch-in-the-ditch around each of the blocks, around the sashing strips, and along the yellow Tri-Mate triangles in the pieced border. Stitch a horizontal and vertical line through the center of each block. Hand-quilt the concentric circles. Machine-quilt a free-motion, meandering design along the sashing strips and blue and green Recs triangles in the pieced border.

Binding: Use a double-fold bias binding cut from the blue fabric; refer to page 79.

Crib Quilt

Size: 42" × 53½"; block, 10" square

Cutting Notes: Dimensions given here for the borders are the mathematical ideal; cut these pieces extra-generously and trim later to accommodate the finished quilt center.

*In the quilt shown, the borders and sashing strips are cut from a juvenile print with a highly directional block design. In a case like this, care must be taken so the design appears right side up throughout, centered along the sashing strips, and so the print is matched at the seams as much as possible. The top and bottom borders strips were cut *first* along the crosswise grain of the fabric. However, the side border strips were cut along the length, to allow for matching the print. Cut out the sashing strips from the fabric that remains from the lengthwise cuts.

**Layer the lavender and pink strips, right sides together with the pink fabric on top, and cut the Recs triangles. The lavender and pink will be in the correct position.

Fabric & Cutting Guide

Element/Fabric	Yardage	First Cut	Second Cut
PINWHEEL BLOCK **Blades/ green print**	¼ yard	5 — 1½" strips	48 Tri-Mate triangles
Inner Blade/lavender print	1¼ yards	2 — 2½" strips**	48 Recs triangles
Outer Blade/pink	¼ yard	2 — 2½" strips**	48 Recs triangles
Background/yellow	⅔ yard	6 — 3½" strips	48 — 3½" × 4½" rectangles
Framing Strips/lavender print		12 — 1½" strips	24 — 1½" × 8½" 24 — 1½" × 10½"
SASHING **Sashing Strips/juvenile print***	1⅔ yard		17 — 1¾" × 10½"
Sashing Squares/lavender		1¾" strip	6 — 1¾" squares
BORDERS/juvenile print*			2 — 5½" × 33" 2 — 5½" × 54¼"
BINDING/lavender print		2¼" bias strips to total 200"	

How-To's

PINWHEEL BLOCK (MAKE 12)

Assemble the blocks, referring to the How-To's for the Lap Quilt, but using the different colors within the block, and only one color (lavender) to frame the block.

QUILT ASSEMBLY

Sashing: Arrange the blocks in 4 rows of 3 blocks in each row. Place a sashing strip between blocks in each row. Press the seam allowances toward the sashing strips.

Assemble 3 rows of horizontal sashing strips, with a sashing square between strips. Press the seam allowances toward the sashing strips. Join the rows of blocks and horizontal sashing strips and sashing squares. Press the seam allowances toward the sashing strip rows.

Border: Stitch a short border strip to the top and bottom of the quilt center. Press the seam allowances toward the border, and trim the ends of the borders even with the quilt center. Stitch a long border strip to each side of the quilt center, matching the print of the top and bottom borders as appropriate. Press the seam allowances toward the borders, and trim the ends of the borders even with the quilt center.

FINISHING SUGGESTIONS

Quilting: Using machine quilting, stitch-in-the-ditch along the green Tri-Mate triangle Pinwheel blades, around each of the blocks inside the framing strips, and along the sashing strips and sashing squares. Hand-quilt lines on the background rectangles of each block, dividing them lengthwise into thirds. Use 1" strips of masking tape to keep the lines straight and evenly spaced. Machine-quilt a free-motion, meandering design along the border.

Binding: Use a lavender, double-fold binding cut on the bias; refer to page 79.

IN FULL BLOOM

Pinwheels on point, framed with broad, leafy patches, call to mind pink magnolias, giant peonies, American Beauty roses, and other lush, oversized blossoms. A pieced floral garland amid deep scallops provides an elegant edging. So effective is the pieced border, it flourishes on a simple quilt that tops a skirted table, a very easy yet elegant project, shown on page 43.

Key Tools: Tri Recs™, Tri-Mate™, Easy
Angle™, Companion Angle™

*Before starting either of these projects,
read through the Tool Tutorial
and the General Directions
for Quiltmaking on pages 68–79, and
the Cutting Notes as well.*

Full-Size Bed Quilt

Size: 82" × 100" – to fit a full or double bed; Pinwheel block, 6"
square

Cutting Notes: *Cut the plain border strips along the length of
the fabric to avoid piecing. Cut them extra-generously; trim them
later to accommodate the finished quilt center and pieced borders. After cutting border strips, use the remaining fabric to cut
the other pieces from the same fabric.

#These are spacer borders; you may wish to pad the width as
well as the length, so as to accommodate the pieced borders (see
page 77 of the General Directions).

**Layer these strips of fabric right sides together with the darker
of the two colors on top, and cut the Companion Angle triangles.
(They are then ready to chain-piece and press as they leave the
cutting mat.)

▾Leave these strips folded right sides together, and cut pairs of
Recs triangles.

Fabric & Cutting Guide			
Element/Fabric Shown	**Yardage**	**First Cut**	**Second Cut**
PLAIN BORDERS*			
Dark pink			2 – 2" × 72½"
			2 – 2" × 57½"
Green			2 – 1¼" × 75½"
			2 – 1¼" × 59"
Pale print			2 – 2¾" × 77"#
			2 – 2¾" × 63½"#
			2 – 5" × 81½"
			2 – 5" × 90½"

(continued)

Fabric & Cutting Guide *(continued)*

Element/Fabric	Yardage	First Cut	Second Cut
PINWHEEL BLOCK			
Pinwheel Petals/light pink	¾ yard	12 — 2" strips	192 Companion Angle triangles**
Pinwheel Petals/medium pink	1⅛ yards	12 — 2" strips	192 Companion Angle triangles**
Background/pale print	5¾ yards	10 — 3½" strips	192 Easy Angle triangles
HOURGLASS UNITS			
Background Triangles/ pale print		9 — 3½" strips	164 Tri triangles
Leaves/green	3½ yards	24 — 2" strips	164 Tri-Mate triangles
HALF HOURGLASS UNITS			
Background Triangles/ pale print		2 — 3½" strips▾	56 Recs triangles (28 pairs)
Leaves/green		4 — 2" strips	28 Tri-Mate triangles
Setting Rectangles and Cornerstones/pale print		3 — 2" strips	24 — 2" × 3½" rectangles 4 — 2" squares
Setting Squares/dark pink	2⅛ yards	3 — 3½" strips	35 — 3½" squares
PIECED BORDER			
Flower Units			
Flower Centers/dark pink		3 — 2⅝" strips	32 — 2⅝" squares
Petals/medium pink		4 — 3½" strips	64 Easy Angle triangles
Background/pale print		4 — 2" strips	64 Companion Angle triangles
Half Hourglass Units			
Background/pale print		2 — 3½" strips▾	64 Recs triangles (32 pairs)
Green		4 — 2" strips	32 Tri-Mate triangles
Leaf Units			
Background/pale print		4 — 3½" strips	28 Tri triangles 28 — 2 × 3½" rectangles
Leaf/green		3 — 3½" strips▾	56 Recs triangles (28 pairs)
Side Leaf Units			
Backround/pale print		1 — 3½" strip▾	8 Recs triangles (4 pairs) 8 — 2" squares
Green		1 — 3½" strip▾	8 Recs triangles (4 pairs)
Cornerstones/pale print		1 — 5" strip	4 — 5" squares
BINDING/green		1¼" bias strips to total 400"	

How To's

QUILT CENTER UNITS

Pinwheel Blocks (make 48): Layer a light- and medium-colored Companion Angle triangle, with right sides together and the medium shade on top. Stitch along the left, and press seam allowances toward the medium colored fabric. Repeat to make a total of 192 triangle units.

Add an Easy Angle triangle cut from a 3½" strip of background fabric to each triangle unit, to form a pieced square as shown in the diagram below. Press the seam allowances on half (96) of these units toward the Easy Angle triangle, and the remaining half toward the petal triangles. This will provide opposing seams when the pieced squares are joined.

Arrange four pieced squares in two rows of two; alternate the way the seam allowances are pressed. Stitch the blocks into rows and press the seam allowances open. Stitch the rows together, and press the seam allowances open.

Hourglass Unit (make 82): Sew a background-fabric Tri triangle to the left side of each green Tri-Mate triangle. Press the seam allowances

toward the Tri-Mate triangle. Combine two of these units to create an Hourglass unit, and press the seam allowances open.

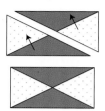

Half Hourglass Unit (make 28 for the quilt center): Stitch a background fabric Recs triangle to the left side of a green Tri-Mate triangle. Press seam allowances towards the Recs triangle. Stitch a background fabric Recs triangle to the right side of the Tri-Mate triangle; this time, press seam allowances toward the the Tri-Mate triangle, to avoid bulk at the intersection of patches.

QUILT CENTER ASSEMBLY

Row A (make 8): Referring to the diagram below, alternate 6 Pinwheel blocks with 5 Hourglass units, and place a half Hourglass unit at each end. Stitch the units together, and press the seam allowances toward the Pinwheel blocks. Make 8 Row A's.

Row B (make 7): Referring to the diagram below, alternate 6 Hourglass units with 5 dark pink setting squares, and place a 2" × 3½" rectangle of background fabric at each end. Stitch the units together, and press the seam allowances toward the setting squares. Make 7 Row B's.

Row C (make 2): Referring to the diagram below, alternate 6 half Hourglass units and 5

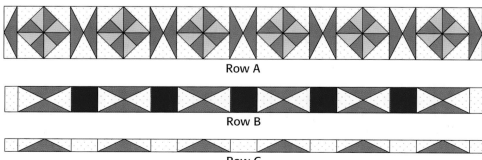

Row A

Row B

Row C

background fabric rectangles, 2" × 3½". Place a 2" square of background fabric at each end. Stitch the units together, and press the seam allowances toward the unpieced sections. Make 2 Row C's.

Assembling the Rows: Arrange the rows, alternating Rows A and B; begin and end with a Row A. Add a Row C to the top and an inverted Row C to the bottom. Stitch the rows together, and press the seam allowances open.

INNER PLAIN BORDERS

Sewing and Pressing: Trim the length of the borders to fit the edge of the quilt top, stitch the borders to the quilt top, and press the seam allowances toward the darker color. First, stitch border strips to the sides of the quilt, then stitch them to the top and bottom. Begin with a 2" border (as shown, dark pink). Next, add a 1¼" border (as shown, green). The outermost plain border (as shown, a pale print) is a spacer border; do not trim or add these strips until after the pieced borders are completed.

PIECED BORDER

Flower Unit: Stitch two Companion Angle triangles cut from the background fabric to two adjacent sides of a 2⅝" square cut from the dark petal fabric. Press seam allowances open to distribute bulk.

Add an Easy Angle triangle cut from the medium petal fabric to each side, pressing towards the Easy Angle triangles to complete the flower. Make 32 half Hourglass units (see page 39); invert and add as shown. Press seam allowances toward the half Hourglass unit to complete the flower unit. Repeat to make 32 flower units.

Side Leaf Unit (make 28): Stitch a Recs triangle cut from the green fabric to the right side of a background Tri triangle, using the "magic angle" to make alignment perfect. Press seam allowances toward the Recs triangle. Add another green fabric Recs triangle to the left side of the Tri unit; this time, press toward the Tri triangle to avoid bulk at the intersection. Stitch a 2" × 3½" rectangle from the background fabric to the bottom to complete the side leaf unit.

End Leaf Unit (make 8): Stitch a Recs triangle of background fabric to a green Recs triangle to form a divided rectangle. Repeat to make 4 for a left end leaf unit, and 4 for a right end leaf unit. Press the seam allowances toward the darker fabrics. Stitch a 2" square of background fabric below each divided rectangle, pressing toward the square.

Left End Leaf Unit   Right End Leaf Unit

Row D (make 2): Arrange a border row, alternating 7 flower units with 6 side leaf units, and place an end leaf unit at each end. Stitch together to form Row D; press seam allowances toward the flower units.

Row E (make 2): Make these pieced borders in the same manner as for Row D, but using 9 flower units. Refer to the side borders in the photo on page 41.

Row D

Assembly: Referring to the General Directions for Spacer Borders on page 76, measure to determine the necessary sizes and cut (or trim) the spacer borders, the outermost plain border strips (as shown, pale print fabric) that will accurately span the distance between the quilt center and the pieced borders. Stitch them to the quilt center—first to the sides, then to the top and bottom. Add a Row E pieced border to each side of the quilt (with the flowers pointing toward the center of the quilt). Add the 5"-square cornerstones to the ends of the Row D pieced borders, then add these borders to the top and bottom of the quilt (with the flowers pointing toward the center of the quilt).

Add a final border of background fabric, 5" wide, first to the sides, then to the top and bottom.

FINISHING SUGGESTIONS

Quilting: Layer and baste the quilt. Quilt by machine with a curvy, large-scaled, overall pattern.

Bound, Scalloped Edge: Once the quilting is completed, mark a repeat of scallops along the edges, with each scallop spanning a flower unit of the pieced border. (*Note:* The Easy Scallop™ tool makes this a simple task.) Machine- or hand-baste along the marked lines. Do not cut on this line, but use the marked line as a guide for positioning the binding for sewing.

Make green, single-fold, bias binding. Beginning at the top of a scallop, stitch ¼" from the edge of the binding until you reach the bottom of the "V." Stop with the needle down, lift the presser foot and pivot the quilt and binding until you can align the edges to sew out of the "V." Continue in this manner around the quilt. Finish the ends, following the directions on page 79. Cut the quilt top, batting, and backing along the stitched scallop. Bring the binding to the backing of the quilt; pin along curves and at the base of each "V" (the binding will naturally fold over upon itself like a reverse mitered corner). Slipstitch the binding in place.

Table Topper

Size: 51" square

How-To's

PIECED BORDERS

Following the How-To's for the Queen-Size Quilt, make 20 flower units, 16 side leaf units, 4 left end leaf units, and 4 right end leaf units. Arrange these units in 4 rows of 5 flower units alternating with 4 side leaf units. Stitch the units together, and press the seam allowances toward the flower units. Each row should measure 42½". If it does not, adjust the inner border strips and the tablecloth center to equal the measurement of your pieced border strips.

Fabric & Cutting Guide

Element/Fabric	Yardage	First Cut	Second Cut
FLOWER UNITS **Flower Centers/** **gold print**	¼ yard	2 — 2⅝" strips	20 squares
Petals/blue print	⅝ yard	2 — 3½" strips	40 Easy Angle triangles
Background/light yellow	1⅛ yards	3 — 2" strips	40 Companion Angle triangles
HALF HOURGLASS UNITS **Leaf/green**	½ yard	3 — 2" strips	20 Tri-Mate triangles
Background/light yellow		2 — 3½" strips	40 Recs triangles (20 pairs)
SIDE & END LEAF UNITS **Leaves/green**		2 — 3½" strips	40 Recs triangles (20 pairs)
Background/light yellow		2 — 3½" strips	16 Tri triangles 8 Recs triangles (4 pairs)
		2 — 2" strips	16 — 2" × 3½" rectangles 8 — 2" squares
		1 — 5" strip	4 — 5" squares
INNER BORDER/light yellow		4 — 2" strips	
TABLECLOTH CENTER/ **large floral print**	1¼ yards	42½" square	
BINDING/blue print		5 — 2¼" strips	

ASSEMBLY

Add a 2" × 42½" plain border strip (cut from the same fabric as the pieced border background) along the top of each pieced border strip. Note the orientation of the flowers, unless you prefer the petals pointing downward. Press the seam allowances toward the plain border strip.

Sew two of these joined borders to opposite sides of the table topper center.

Assemble 4 corner blocks as shown at right, and add one to each end of the remaining pieced borders.

Press toward the corner blocks.

Sew these borders to the remaining two sides of the table topper center. To provide an interesting angle to the corners of the table topper, cut the corner blocks on the diagonal as shown in the diagram at right.

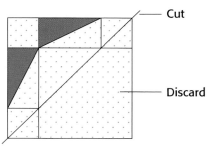

Table Topper Corner

FINISHING SUGGESTIONS

Quilting: Layer with a thin batting (or none at all) and baste. Machine-quilt a 3" grid in the center. Quilt ¼" outside the seams of the flower/leaf units.

Binding: Use double-fold binding cut along the straight-of-grain; refer to page 79.

COME OVER TO MY HOUSE

Y ou'll love creating a neighborhood of House blocks. For a lively look, alternate the direction of the roofs' slopes. Or, adopt a whimsical plan of randomly sloping rooflines and a scrap-quilt mix of fabrics, as shown in the wall-hanging version of this design on page 51.

Key Tool: Tri-Recs™

> *Before starting either of these projects,*
> *read through the Tool Tutorial*
> *and the General Directions*
> *for Quiltmaking on pages 68–79, and*
> *the Cutting Notes as well.*

Lap Quilt

Size: 63" × 78"; House block, 9" square (not including Log Cabin framing strips)

Cutting Notes: *Cut the border strips along the length of the fabric to avoid piecing. Cut them extra-generously; trim them later to accommodate the finished quilt center.

▾Cut the inner border strips first (red fabric), then use the remaining fabric to cut the other pieces from the same fabric.

Fabric & Cutting Guide

Element/Fabric Shown	Yardage	First Cut	Second Cut
HOUSE BLOCKS			
Sky/tan	½ yard	1 — 6½" strip 1 — 2" strip	12 Recs triangles (6 pairs) 12 — 2" x 3½" rectangles
Roof/brown	⅜ yard	1 — 6½" strip 1 — 3½" strip	12 Recs triangles (6 pairs) 12 — 3½" squares
Chimney/stone print	⅛ yard	1 — 2" strip	12 — 2" × 3½" rectangles
Doors, Windows/gold	½ yard	3 — 2¾" strips	12 — 2¾" × 5" rectangles 12 — 2¾" squares
House Front/red	2 yards	1 — 2¾" strips	12 — 2¾" squares 24 — 2" × 5" rectangles
		8 — 2" strips	12 — 2" × 6½" rectangles 12 — 2" × 2¾" rectangles 12 — 2" × 5¾" rectangles
Log Cabin Framing Strips			
Green	⅝ yard	1 — 9½" strip 1 — 11" strip	12 — 2" × 9½" rectangles 12 — 2" × 11" rectangles
Blue	⅝ yard	1 — 9 ½" strip 1 — 11" strip	12 — 2" × 9½" rectangles 12 — 2" × 11" rectangles

(continued)

Fabric & Cutting Guide *(continued)*

Element/Fabric	Yardage	First Cut	Second Cut
Log Cabin Framing Strips *(continued)*			
Dark green	1 yard	1 — 12½" strip	12 — 2" × 12½" rectangles
		1 — 14" strip	12 — 2" × 14" rectangles
Dark blue	1 yard	1 — 12½" strip	12 — 2" × 12½" rectangles
		1 — 14" strip	12 — 2" × 14" rectangles
Cornerstones/gold		3 — 2" strips	48 — 2" squares
BORDER STRIPS & STARS			
Star blocks			
Background/tan		2 — 2½" strips	16 Tri triangles
			16 squares
Star Points/red		1 — 2½" strip	32 Recs triangles (16 pairs)
Center/gold		1 — 2½" strip	4 squares
Log Cabin Framing Strips			
Cornerstones/gold		1 — 2" strip	8 — 2" squares
Framing Strips/dark green		2 — 2" strips	4 — 2" × 6½" rectangles
			4 — 2" × 8" rectangles
Framing Strips/dark blue		2 — 2" strips	4 — 2" × 6½" rectangles
			4 — 2" × 8" rectangles
Inner Border/red*▾			2 — 2" × 60½" rectangles
			2 — 2" × 45½" rectangles
Outer Border/plaid*	2 yards		2 — 8" × 45½" rectangles
			2 — 8" × 60½" rectangles
BINDING/red		9 — 2¼" strips from remaining width to total 294"	

How-To's

HOUSE BLOCK (MAKE 12)

Roof/Sky: Stitch together a Recs triangle cut from roof fabric and one from sky fabric to make a divided rectangle unit. As cut, half the roofs will slope to the right, and half will slope to the left. Press as shown.

Stitch together a rectangle of chimney fabric with a rectangle of sky fabric to form a square. Draw a diagonal line on the wrong side of the roof square. Layer these pieces right sides together, and stitch on the marked line. Trim the excess fabric, leaving ¼" seam allowances. Press.

Join a chimney/roof square and a divided rectangle roof section to make a complete roof/sky unit. Press seam allowances open. Repeat to make 12 roof/sky units.

House Front: Referring to the diagram, join pieces B, C (window), and D; stitch E and G to each side of door F, and add lintel H. Join the units together, pressing as you go.

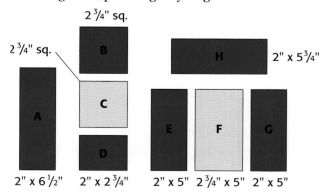

2¾" sq.

2¾" sq.

B

H   2" x 5¾"

A

C

E   F   G

D

2" x 6½"   2" x 2¾"   2" x 5"   2¾" x 5"   2" x 5"

Block Assembly: Sew the roof unit to the bottom portion of the house; press. The completed House block should measure 9½", including seam allowances.

Log Cabin Framing Strips: Arrange "logs" and cornerstones around each House block as shown in the diagrams below.

Using green fabric, stitch a 2" × 9½" log to the left side of each House block, then a 2" × 11" log to the bottom edge. Press toward the logs.

Stitch a cornerstone to one side of each blue log. Press toward the log. Stitch the shorter one to the right side of the block, and the longer one on the top of the block. Press toward the logs.

Add the dark green and dark blue logs in the same way, completing the block. At this point the house block with the framing strips should measure 15½", including seam allowances.

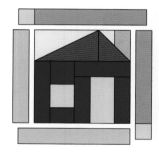
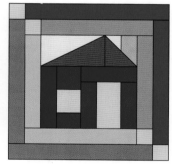

QUILT CENTER ASSEMBLY

Arrangement: Arrange the House blocks in 4 rows of 3 blocks. Experiment with different layouts until you are satisfied with the balance of roofs that slope to the left and roofs that slope to the right.

Sewing & Pressing: Stitch the blocks together into rows; press the seam allowances in alternating directions. Sew the rows together, taking care to match the corners. Press seam allowances in one direction.

The quilt center should measure 45½" × 60½" at this point.

BORDERS

Star Block (make 4): Assemble the Tri-Recs units by sewing a Recs unit to the right side of the Tri unit. Press towards the Recs unit. Add another Recs unit to the left side of the Tri unit. Press. Repeat to make 4 Tri-Recs units for each Star block.

Arrange the Star block using the 4 Tri-Recs units, 4 squares for the corners, and a contrast square for the center. Sew a corner square to each side of the top and bottom Tri-Recs units. Press seam allowances as shown. Sew the center square between the remaining 2 Tri-Recs units. Press as shown. Join the 3 rows to complete the block, and press seam allowances outward. Each Star block should measure 6½". Repeat to make 4 Star blocks.

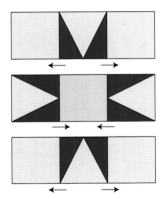

Sew the Log Cabin framing strips to the Star blocks in the same manner as for the House blocks. See below for placement. Press. At this point the Star block should measure 9½" square, including seam allowances.

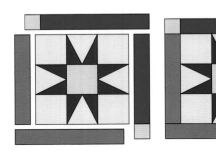

BORDER STRIPS:

Sew the corresponding inner and outer border strips for each side of the quilt together, creating 9½"-wide pieced border strips. Trim the shorter pieced borders to the same size as the top and bottom of the quilt center, stitch them in place, and press the seam allowances toward the outer border strips.

Trim the remaining pieced border strips to the same length as the quilt center (including seam allowances), and sew a Star block to each end. Sew to the sides of the quilt and press the seam allowances toward the outer border strips.

FINISHING SUGGESTIONS

Quilting: Stitch-in-the-ditch by machine or by hand around the door, window, and roof and around the House block. Stitch-in-the-ditch between the sashing strips. Quilt the border, following the lines of the plaid.

Binding: Use a red, double-fold binding cut on the straight of grain.

Embellishment: For doorknobs, sew on buttons ½" in diameter.

Crib Quilt or Wall Hanging

Size: 46" × 56"; House block, 6" square (not including Log Cabin sashing)

Cutting Notes: Cut the border strips first; cut them extra-generously; trim them later to accommodate the finished quilt center. Use remaining fabric to cut the patches for the sky, and backgrounds for the Star blocks.

Likewise, cut the sashing strips first, then use the remaining fabrics to cut other pieces, resulting in a good variety of prints and colors throughout for the roofs, chimneys, and house fronts of the House blocks, and for the points, centers, and Log Cabin sashing of the Star blocks. You will need a total of 1¾ yards for these pieces.

For the pieced, scrap-look binding, see the How-To's on page 51.

Fabric & Cutting Guide

Element/Fabric Shown	Yardage	First Cut	Second Cut
HOUSE BLOCKS **Sky/yellow**	1⅝ yard	1 — 4½" strip 1 — 1½" strip	12 Recs triangles (6 pairs) 12 — 1½" × 2½" rectangles
Chimney/variety		1 — 1½" strip	12 — 1½" × 2½" rectangles
For Each Block: **House Front/variety**			1 — 1½" × 4½" rectangle 1 — 1½" × 4" rectangle 2 — 1½" × 3½" rectangles 1 — 1½" × 2" rectangle 1 — 2" square
Doors, Windows/variety			1 — 2" × 3½" rectangle 1 — 2" square
Roof/variety		4½" strip	12 Recs triangles (cut in pairs) 12 — 2½" squares
Log Cabin Framing Strips **Cornerstones/bright yellow**		2 — 1½" strips	48 — 1½" squares
Light green	¼ yard	1 — 7½" strip	12 — 1½" × 7½" rectangles 12 — 1½" × 6½" rectangles
Light blue	¼ yard	1 — 7½" strip	12 — 1½" × 7½" rectangles 12 — 1½" × 6½" rectangles
Dark green	⅜ yard	1 — 9½" strip	12 — 1½" × 9½" rectangles 12 — 1½" × 8½" rectangles
Dark blue	⅜ yard	1 — 9½" strip	12 — 1½" × 9½" rectangles 12 — 1½" × 8½" rectangles

(continued)

Fabric & Cutting Guide *(continued)*

Element/Fabric Shown	Yardage	First Cut	Second Cut
BORDER STRIPS & STARS **Border Strips/yellow**		4 — 8½" strips	2 — 8½" × 30½" rectangles 2 — 8½" × 20½" rectangles 4 — 2½" × 8½" rectangles
Star Background/yellow		4 — 2½" strips	32 — 2½" squares 32 Tri triangles
Star Points/variety		2½" strips	64 Recs triangles (32 pairs)
Star Centers/variety			8 — 2½" squares
Framing Strips/variety		1½" strips	16 — 1½" × 6½" rectangles 16 — 1½" × 7½" rectangles
Cornerstones/gold		1 — 1½" strip	16 — 1½" squares
BINDING/variety	remnants	2½" strips	

How-To's

HOUSE BLOCKS (MAKE 12)

Assemble the House blocks, referring to the How-To's for the Lap Quilt, but using the measurements for the house front pieces as shown below:

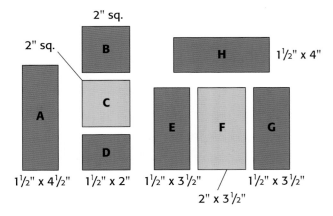

Vary the fabrics for all but the sky pieces, and vary the slants of the roofs. This can be done by simply layering two different fabric strips for the roofs right sides together when the Rec triangles are cut. One Recs triangle will face

one direction and the second one will face the opposite direction. The completed House blocks should measure 6½" square, including seam allowances. Add Log Cabin sashing strips and cornerstones in the same way as for the Lap Quilt.

QUILT CENTER ASSEMBLY

Assemble the quilt center, referring to the How-To's for the Lap Quilt; experiment with different layouts until you find one with a mix of colors and rooflines that you like.

At this point the quilt center should measure 30½" × 40½".

BORDERS

Star Block (make 8): Assemble 8 Star blocks referring to the How-To's for the lap quilt. The Star blocks should measure 6½" with seam allowances. Add the sashing strips, same as for the lap quilt. The block should now measure 8½" square.

Border Assembly: *Note:* Adjust measurements as needed so borders fit your Star blocks and your quilt center.

For the top border, stitch a 2½" × 8½" border rectangle, a Star block, and an 8½" × 20½" border rectangle in a row. Press seam allowances toward the borders. Repeat for the bottom border. Sew to the top and bottom of the quilt center.

For the side borders, stitch a Star block, a 2½" × 8½" border rectangle, a Star block, an 8½" × 30½" border rectangle, and another Star block in a row. Press seam allowances toward the borders. Sew to the sides of the quilt center. Press seam allowances toward the borders.

FINISHING SUGGESTIONS

Quilting: Using #8 pearl cotton in yellow, stitch-in-the-ditch, following the lines of the houses and sashes. Use a variegated pearl cotton to stitch a design in the border, using Sliding Stencil #8827003.

Binding: Sew 2½" straight-of-grain strips of various fabrics together to form a strip set. Cut this strip set into 1¼" bias strips. Join the strips to make single-fold, bias binding, 216" in length. Sew it around the quilt; refer to page 79.

PINE GROVE

The classic Pine Tree block branches off in a fresh, new direction with treetop boughs cut using the wide angle of the Tri-Mate™ tool. Framing each block in an on-point square and providing a color palette of natural woodsy hues results in a handsome lap quilt. Need a quick and easy project with which to deck the hall for the holidays? Jack Frost will help you paint just a trio of Pine Tree blocks in silvery blue and white prints; see page 57 for that project.

Key Tools: Recs™, Tri-Mate™, Easy Angle™

> *Before starting either of these projects,
> read through the Tool Tutorial
> and the General Directions
> for Quiltmaking on pages 68–79.*

Lap Quilt

Size: 51" × 62"; Pine Tree block, 6" square (not including
framing triangles)

Cutting Notes: *Cut the outer border strips *first* along the length
of the fabric to avoid piecing. Cut them extra-generously; trim
them later to accommodate the finished quilt center. Use remaining fabric to cut strips, first for the framing triangles, then for the
Tri-Mate treetops pieces. Cut the inner borders across the width.

**These Easy Angle triangles are cut larger than needed; they
will be trimmed after piecing.

▾These pieces will be sewn first to make a strip set, then cut for
the trunk unit; see the How-To's on page 54.

Fabric & Cutting Guide

Element/Fabric Shown	Yardage	First Cut	Second Cut
BORDERS			
Inner Borders*/brown	⅜ yard	5 — 2" strips	2 — 2" × 48½" (pieced) 2 — 2" × 39½"
Outer Borders*/green	1⅝ yards		2 — 6" × 51½" 2 — 6" × 53½"
PINE TREE BLOCKS			
Framing Triangles/dark green	1½ yards	4 — 5" strips	48 Easy Angle triangles**
Framing Triangles/green		5" strips	24 Easy Angle triangles**
Treetops/green		2" strips	36 Tri-Mate triangles
Treetops/dark green		3 — 2" strips	18 Tri-Mate triangles
Treetops Background/ecru	⅔ yard	4 — 3½" strips	108 Recs triangles (54 pairs)
Tree Trunk/brown		1 — 1½" strip▾	
Tree Trunk Background/ecru		2 — 3" strips▾	
SETTING TRIANGLES/tan	⅞ yard	3 — 14" squares	Cut in half twice diagonally to yield 12 quarter-square triangles
		2 — 7½" squares	Cut in half once diagonally to yield 4 half-square triangles
BINDING/dark green		2¼" bias strips to total 236"	

How-To's

PINE TREE BLOCK (MAKE 18)

Treetop Tiers: Sew a Recs triangle cut from the background fabric to the left side of a Tri-Mate triangle cut from the lighter treetop fabric. Press the seam allowances toward the darker fabric. Complete the unit by adding a Recs triangle cut from the background fabric to the right side of the Tri-Mate triangle. Press

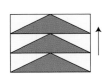

the seam allowances as before. Repeat to make 36 pieced treetop tiers using the lighter treetops fabric, and 18 using the darker shade.

Treetop Unit: Stitch 3 pieced treetop tiers of the same treetop fabric together to make the

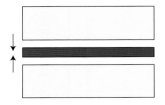

boughs of the tree block. Press the seam allowances upward, toward the top of the block.

Tree Trunk: Stitch a 3" strip of background fabric to each side of a 1½" strip of trunk fabric to form a strip set. Press the seam allowances toward the trunk fabric. Cut this strip set into 2" tree trunk sections, one for each of the 18 blocks.

2"
sections

Complete the blocks by sewing a tree trunk section to each treetop unit. Press the seam allowances toward the tree trunk. At this point, the block should measure 6 ½" square.

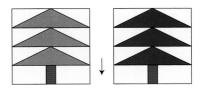

Framing Triangles: Use the alternate treetops fabric, so the framing triangles contrast with the treetops of each individual block. Sew an Easy Angle triangle to opposite sides of the tree blocks, lining up the center of the pieced block with the point of the Easy Angle so equal amounts hang out over the sides. Press the seam allowances toward the Easy Angle triangles. Sew an Easy Angle triangle to the remaining sides in the same manner, and press as before. Trim the blocks, squaring them up and leaving just ¼" seam allowance beyond the background fabric corners of the Pine Tree block. Each block at this point should measure the same size, just shy of 9" square.

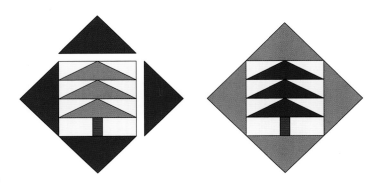

QUILT CENTER ASSEMBLY

Arrangement: Working on a design wall, arrange the quilt blocks on point. Referring to the photograph on the opposite page, start with a horizontal row of 3 blocks on point, each featuring the lighter color treetop and the darker color framing triangles. Center two blocks with the reverse color scheme below that. Continue to alternate the on-point rows, ending as you began.

Setting Triangles: Cut the 14" squares (as shown here, in tan fabric) in half twice diagonally to form 12 quarter-square triangles. Place these along the sides to square up the quilt. Cut the 7½" squares in half once diagonally to form 4 half-square triangles; place one of these in each corner.

Sewing & Pressing: Stitch the blocks and setting triangles together in diagonal rows. Press the seam allowances open. Stitch the rows together;

press the seam allowances all in one direction. Trim the edges of the quilt center square, leaving just ¼" beyond the corners of the blocks.

BORDERS

Inner Border: Using the same fabric as for the tree trunks, piece the 2" strips as needed to obtain the inner borders of the required length. First stitch these to the sides, trimming the ends even with the quilt center. Press seam allowances toward the border. Add inner borders to the top and bottom and press as before.

Outer Border: Add the wider border strips in the same way as for the inner border.

FINISHING SUGGESTIONS

Quilting: Layer and baste the quilt. Machine-quilt the center: Stitch-in-the-ditch along each treetop tier and tree trunk, and around the unframed and the framed Pine Tree block. Create a 1" diagonal grid where 4 framing triangles come together to form a square. Use free-motion quilting to create free-form pine boughs, pinecones, and berries along the borders and setting triangles.

Binding: Use double-fold bias binding, referring to page 79.

Winter Pines Wall Hanging

Size: 14½" × 28¾"; Pine Tree block,
4" square (not including framing triangles)

Key Tools: Tri-Mate™, Tri-Recs™,
Companion Angle™, Easy Angle™

How To's

PINE TREE BLOCKS (MAKE 3)

Pine Tree Unit: Referring to the How-To's for the lap quilt, assemble the treetop units. For the tree trunk units, stitch a tree trunk square between 2 tree trunk background rectangles. Stitch a treetop and tree trunk unit together; press toward the top of the block. Each Pine Tree unit should measure 4½" square, including seam allowances.

Framing Triangles: Sew an Easy Angle triangle to opposite sides of the tree blocks, lining up the center of the pieced block with the point of the Easy Angle so equal amounts hang out over the sides. Press the seam allowances toward the Easy Angle triangles. Sew an Easy Angle triangle to the remaining sides in the same man-

Fabric & Cutting Guide

Element/Fabric Shown	Yardage	First Cut	Second Cut
PINE TREE BLOCKS			
Treetops/silvery white	¼ yard	1 — 1½" strip	9 Tri-Mate triangles
Treetops Background/dark blue	¼ yard	1 — 2½" strip	18 Recs triangles (9 pairs)
Tree Trunk/gray	scraps		3 — 1½" squares
Tree Trunk background/dark blue		2" strip	6 — 1½" × 2" rectangles
Framing Triangles/blue	½ yard	1 — 3½" strip	12 Easy Angle triangles
SETTING TRIANGLES/silvery white		1 — 5" strip	4 Companion Angle triangles 4 Easy Angle triangles
BORDERS **Inner Borders/dark blue**		2 — 1½" strips	2 — 1½" × 22½" 2 — 1½" × 10"
Outer Borders*/blue		2 — 3" strips	2 — 3" × 24½" 2 — 3" × 14½"
BINDING/blue		1¼" strips to total 96"	

ner, and press as before. Trim the blocks, squaring them up and leaving just ¼" seam allowance beyond the background fabric corners of the Pine Tree block. Each block at this point should measure 5¾" square.

ASSEMBLY

Arrangement: Referring to the photo, arrange the Pine Tree blocks in a vertical row. Fill in with setting triangles.

Sewing & Pressing: Refer to the How-To's for the lap quilt to join the setting triangles and blocks in diagonal rows, press, trim the setting triangles (which are also larger than needed), and add the inner and outer border strips.

FINISHING SUGGESTIONS

Quilting: Layer and baste the quilt. Using hand quilting and dark blue thread, stitch-in-the-ditch around each tree, the Pine Tree unit, the block, and between the borders. Measure and mark a double zigzag along the border, then quilt. Using pale blue-gray thread, hand-quilt swirl designs in the setting triangles.

Binding: Use 1¼" single-fold binding; refer to page 79.

HOMECOMING SAMPLER

Try out lots of patterns from this book while you create a charming folk art scene. The sum is greater than the parts, yet each part is easy: a starlit sky, a clearing in the woods, a cozy cabin with a pond and a flower garden right out the front door. Novelty and vintage buttons add rewards for anyone who takes a closer look. Fun to make, this wall hanging will surely warm your heart and your home.

Key Tools: Tri-Recs™, Tri-Mate™, Easy Angle™, Companion Angle™

Size: 45" square

> *Before starting this project,*
> *read through the Tool Tutorial*
> *and the General Directions*
> *for Quiltmaking on pages 68–79,*
> *and the Cutting Notes as well.*

Fabric Needed:

Dark gold (Stars): ¼ yard
Light gold (Stars): ¼ yard
Dark blue (Sky Background): ⅝ yard
Medium green (Woodsy Background): 1 yard
Brown print (Roof): scrap
Stone print (Chimney, Path): ⅛ yard
Brown stripe (Door, Tree Trunks): ⅛ yard
Red (House, Inner Border): ½ yard
Golden brown (Window): scrap
Dark green floral (Treetop #1): ⅛ yard
Dark green speckled (Treetop #2): ⅛ yard
Mauve print (Fish): ⅛ yard
Pale gold (Fish): ⅛ yard
Blue (Water): ¼ yard
Sage green (Grassy Background): ½ yard
Pink (Petals): ⅛ yard
Yellow (Flower Centers): scraps
Red plaid (Flying Geese): ⅜ yard
Brown (Binding): ¼ yard

Night Sky Section

Cutting Notes: *Layer the strips *right sides up,* and cut the following combinations of Recs triangles:

6 Divided rectangles of dark gold and blue
4 Divided rectangles of light gold and blue
20 Divided rectangles of dark gold and light gold

   6   4   20

How-To's

Refer to the How-To's for the Yankee Doodle Stars lap quilt on page 18 to make the star point units of divided Recs rectangles, the wide rows of background squares and vertical star points, and the narrow rows of star points and star centers. Assemble the rows according to the diagram on page 60.

Note that the wide rows end in a large Easy Angle triangle (dark blue, as shown) on the left side. Press the seam allowances toward the squares, large or small, or toward the Easy Angle triangle.

Fabric & Cutting Guide

Element/Fabric Shown	Yardage	First Cut	Second Cut
Stars Points/dark gold	¼ yard	1 — 3½" strip	26 Recs* triangles
Star Centers/dark gold		1 — 2" strip	9 — 2" squares
Stars Points/light gold	¼ yard	1 — 3½" strips	24 Recs* triangles
Star Centers/light gold		1 — 2" strip	6 — 2" squares
Sky Background/dark blue	⅝ yard (includes borders)	2 — 3½" strips	15 — 3½" squares 6 Easy Angle triangles 10 — Recs* triangles

Join the rows together, and press the seam allowances toward the wide rows. Once the Night Sky Section is pieced and pressed, trim the squares at the left side of each narrow row even with the Easy Angle triangles to obtain a straight, diagonal edge.

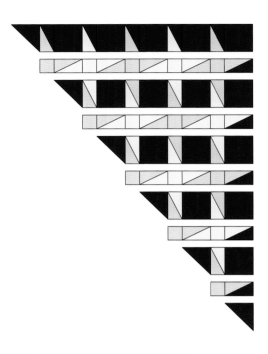

Cabin Block

Cutting Notes: *Set aside remaining red print fabric to be used for the spacer border as the quilt is being assembled.

**These will be sewn together to form the roof. Layer the roof (brown) fabric and the background (medium green) fabrics with the right sides up and with the background fabric on top to cut the Recs triangles.

Fabric & Cutting Guide

Element/Fabric Shown	Yardage	First Cut	Second Cut
Woodsy Background/medium green	1 yard total (includes pieces used in other sections)	1 — 6½" strip	1 Recs triangle** 1 — 2" × 3½" rectangle
Roof/brown shingle print	scrap	1 — 6½" strip	1 Recs triangle** 1 — 3½" square
Chimney/stone print	scrap		1 — 2" × 3½" rectangle
Door/brown stripe (includes tree trunks)	⅛ yard		1 — 2¾" × 5" rectangle
House Front/red print*	½ yard	1 — 2¾" strip	1 — 2" × 6½" rectangle 2 — 2" × 5" rectangles 1 — 2" × 5¾" rectangle 1 — 2¾" square 1 — 2" × 2¾" rectangle
Window/golden brown	scrap		1 — 2¾" square

How To's

Refer to the How-To's for the Come Over to My House lap quilt on page 46 to assemble one 9" square house. Note that for this design, the background fabric that combines with the roof pieces is the forest floor (a medium green fern print, as shown) rather than a fabric representative of the sky.

Pine Tree Blocks
How-To's

Refer to the How-To's for the Pine Grove lap quilt on page 54, and assemble 7 Pine Tree blocks, each 6½" square including seam allowances. Make 5 blocks with treetops in one fabric, and 2 blocks with treetops in the other fabric.

Fabric & Cutting Guide

Element/Fabric Shown	Yardage	First Cut	Second Cut
Woodsy Background Treetops/ medium green		2 — 3½" strips	42 Recs triangles (21 pairs)
Woodsy Background Tree Trunk/ medium green		1 — 3" strip	
Treetop #1/dark green floral	⅛ yard	2 — 2" strips	15 Tri-Mate triangles
Treetop #2/dark green speckled	⅛ yard	1 — 2" strip	6 Tri-Mate triangles
Tree Trunk/brown stripe		1 — 1½" strip	

Cabin & Woods Section

Cutting Notes: Use the chart below to cut the additional pieces for setting the blocks together. The triangles are slightly larger than needed and will be trimmed just before the Night Sky Section is added.

Fabric & Cutting Guide

Element/Fabric Shown	Yardage	First Cut	Second Cut
Woodsy Background/medium green		1 — 8" strip	1 — 8" square, cut in half once diagonally to yield 2 triangles
			2 — 3½" × 8" rectangles
		1 — 6½" strip	2 — Easy Angle triangles
			2 — 6½" squares
			5 — 2" × 6½" rectangles
			1 — 5" × 6½" rectangle
		1 — 3½" strip	1 — 3½" × 18½" rectangle

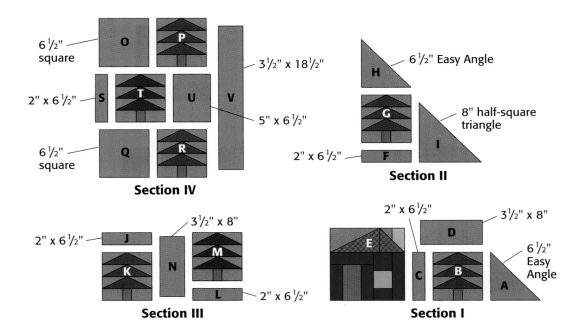

6½" square — O, P

3½" x 18½"

2" x 6½" — S, T, U, V

5" x 6½"

6½" square — Q, R

Section IV

6½" Easy Angle — H

8" half-square triangle — G, I

2" x 6½" — F

Section II

2" x 6½" — J

3½" x 8"

K, N, M

2" x 6½" — L

Section III

2" x 6½" — E

3½" x 8" — D

6½" Easy Angle — A

C, B

Section I

How To's

Referring to the diagrams above, arrange and assemble the pieces in each Section (starting with I and proceeding to IV), following an alphabetical order within each Section. Whenever possible, press the seam allowances toward the piece with the fewest seams along its edge.

Join Sections I and II, join Sections III and IV, and then stitch the joined Sections together. Press as before.

When the entire Cabin and Woods Section is completed, trim the edge evenly at a 45-degree angle. Sew the Cabin and Woods Section to the Night Sky Section, taking care not to stretch the bias edges.

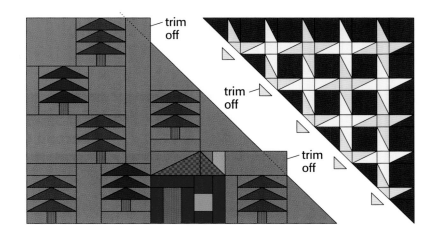

trim off

trim off

trim off

Fish Pond Section

Cutting Notes: *Place strips right sides together to get pairs of Recs triangles.

Fabric & Cutting Guide

Element/Fabric Shown	Yardage	First Cut	Second Cut
Tailfins/mauve print	⅛ yard	1 — 2" strip	10 Recs triangles (5 pairs)*
Top & Bottom Fins/mauve print		1 — 1¼" strip	10 — 1¼" squares
Fish Heads/pale gold	⅛ yard	1 — 2" strip	5 Easy Angle triangles
Fish Bodies/mauve print		1 — 2" strip	5 Easy Angle triangles
Water/blue	¼ yard	1 — 4½" strip	4 Companion Angles 1 Easy Angle triangle
		2 — 2" strips	5 — 2" × 5" rectangles 5 — 2" × 3½" rectangles 5 — 2" squares 10 Recs triangles (5 pairs)* 10 — 1¼" × 2" rectangles
Grassy Background/sage green	½ yard (includes pieces used in other sections)		2 — 4½" Easy Angle triangles
Woodsy Background/medium green			1 — 4½" Easy Angle triangle

How-To's

Refer to the How-To's for the Big & Little Fishies quilt on page 25 to assemble 5 fish blocks, each 3" square. Add sashing to two adjacent sides of each block using the 2" × 3½" rectangles and the 2" × 5" rectangles.

Assemble the Fish Pond Section in diagonal rows, adding the Easy Angle triangles to the corners. Place the woodsy background Easy Angle triangle (medium green) in the upper left-hand corner. Place the two grassy background Easy Angle triangles (sage green) at the upper right corner and the lower right corner. Use the Companion Angle triangles to fill in each edge. These triangles are all larger than needed. After piecing, trim the entire section to a rectangle measuring 14" wide and 12½" tall.

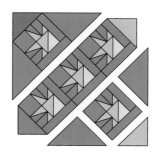

Flower Garden Section

Element/Fabric Shown	Yardage	First Cut	Second Cut
Fabric & Cutting Guide			
Grassy Background/sage green		3 — 2" strips	1 — 2" × 11" rectangle 2 — 2" × 5" rectangles 4 — 2" × 3½" rectangles 24 — 2" squares 56 Recs triangles (28 pairs)
Petals/pink	⅛ yard	2 — 2" strips	28 Tri triangles
Inner Flower Centers/pink		1 — 2" strip	7 — 2" squares
Outer Flower Centers/ yellow	scraps	1 — 1¼" strip	28 — 1¼" squares

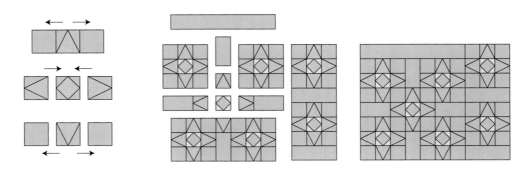

Path Section

Element/Fabric Shown	Yardage	First Cut	Second Cut
Fabric & Cutting Guide			
Grassy background/sage green		1 — 3 ½" strip	2 — 3½" × 6½" rectangles 4 Easy Angle triangles 2 Companion Angle triangles
Path/stone print	⅛ yard	1 — 3½" strip	4 Easy Angle triangles 2 Companion Angle triangles

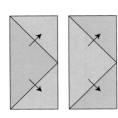 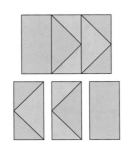 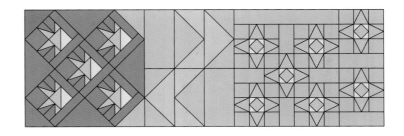

How To's

Note: This section features the same flowers as shown in the Charlotte's Garden wall hanging on page 6, but uses a different setting and assembly technique.

Petals: Make 28 Tri-Recs units: For each, sew a Recs triangle to the right side of the Tri triangle, using the "magic angle" to make alignment perfect. Press seam allowances toward the Recs triangle. Add another Recs triangle to the left side of the Tri unit. Press seam allowances toward the Recs triangle.

Flower Centers: Make 7 of the Square-in-a-Square units as in Charlotte's Garden; refer to page 8. Alter the size as follows: Use a 2" square for the larger square, which becomes the center of the Square-in-a-Square unit. Use 1¼" squares for the 4 surrounding squares, to create the corners.

Block Assembly: Sew together 6 flower blocks; for each, arrange 4 Tri-Recs units, a Square-in-a-Square, and 4 grassy background squares. Join in rows, pressing as shown in the diagram at far left on the opposite page. Join the rows, and press the seam allowances toward the upper and lower rows.

Section Assembly: Arrange the remaining Tri-Recs units, Square-in-a-Square unit, and the grassy background rectangles into two sections, as shown in the middle of the opposite page. For the section containing 5 flowers, sew a short rectangle to each separate Tri-Recs unit, to form a unit. Join the units into rows, then join the rows together; whenever possible, press the seam allowances toward the rectangles. Assemble the section containing 2 flowers, then combine the two sections to complete the Flower Garden Section.

How-To's

Flying Geese Units: To assemble a Flying Goose unit, sew an Easy Angle triangle to the right side of a Companion Angle triangle. Press the seam allowances toward the Easy Angle triangle. Add another Easy Angle triangle to the left side of the Companion Angle triangle. Press the seam allowances toward the Easy Angle triangle. Make 2 Flying Geese units using the 2 contrasting fabrics; then make 2 more, reversing the positions of the fabrics.

Section Assembly: Referring to the diagram at the bottom center on the opposite page, arrange the Flying Geese units and the grassy background rectangles together to form both halves of the section, and then join the 2 halves to complete the section. Whenever possible, press the seam allowances toward the piece with the fewest seams along its edge.

Quilt Center Assembly

Referring to the diagram at bottom right on the opposite page, join the Path Section to the Flower Garden Section. Add the Fish Pond Section.

Measure the combined piece, and trim along the left side if necessary so that it matches the top of the design in width (the cabin, woods, and night sky). Stitch these two major parts together to complete the quilt center.

Borders and Binding

Fabric & Cutting Guide			
Element/Fabric Shown	**Yardage**	**First Cut**	**Second Cut**
Flying Geese/red plaid	⅜ yard	3 — 3½" strips	56 Tri triangles
Flying Geese Background/dark blue		4 — 3½" strips	112 Recs triangles (56 pairs)
BINDING/BROWN	¼ yard	5 — 1¼" strips to total 190"	

How To's

Pieced Border Strips: Referring to the How-To's for the Woven Geese queen-size quilt on page 13, make 56 Tri-Recs units for the border. Sew 13 of these units together into a strip for each of the 4 sides of the quilt top. Reserve the remaining 4 units for now.

Assembly: Use the (red) fabric you set aside before cutting the pieces for the Cabin walls as spacer border strips. Referring to the General Directions for Spacer Borders on page 76, measure to determine the necessary sizes and cut the spacer border strips, so that they will span the distance between the quilt center and the pieced borders. Stitch the spacer borders to the quilt center, first to the sides and then to the top and bottom. Press the seam allowances toward the spacer borders.

Working on a design wall or a large surface, arrange the pieced border strips so that the Flying Geese "fly" around the quilt continuously. Refer to the black and white diagram and to the photo of the quilt on page 58. Stitch 2 of the pieced borders to the sides of the quilt. Stitch the remaining Tri-Recs units to the ends of the remaining pieced border strips, paying close attention to the direction each Flying Goose is headed. Stitch these border strips to the top and bottom of the quilt.

FINISHING SUGGESTIONS

Quilting: Layer and baste the quilt. Stitch-in-the-ditch around each motif and around the pieced border. In the Night Sky Section, use yellow topstitching thread to straight-stitch lines, or rays of starlight, radiating from the upper right corner out to the hill. In the Cabin & Woods Section, quilt several Tri-Mate, or treetop, shapes to fill in the open spaces around the Pine Tree blocks and to suggest more trees in the background. Using a decorative zigzag stitch, quilt in horizontal rows along the cabin walls to suggest logs. Using a fine satin stitch, outline the door and window of the cabin; add crossbars over the window for windowpanes. In the Fish Pond Section, use a decorative stitch to machine-embroider a line of scallops alongside the seam between each fish head and fish body. Use free-motion stitching to quilt swirly waves in the water of the pond. In the Path Section, outline the stones in the printed fabric of the path itself. In the Flower Garden Section, echo-quilt in curves around each flower petal, and stitch vertical lines over the entire grassy background.

Binding: Use a single-fold straight-of-grain binding, referring to page 79; include a sleeve for hanging your quilt.

Embellishments: For the smoke coming from the chimney, braid strands of #8 pearl cotton, and couch the braid to secure it in place on the background in graceful curves and loops. Sew on various buttons: Sprinkle 2 sizes of star-shaped buttons over the Night Sky section. Sew a small (3/8" to 1/2") round button to the center of each flower and to the door, for a doorknob. Sew a tiny doll button to each fish head, for an eye. Add novelty buttons: birds on the trees, a cat in the window.

TOOL TUTORIAL

This section is devoted to the use of the key tools used in this book: the Tri™ and Recs™ that come packaged together as the Tri-Recs™ tools, the Tri-Mate™, the Easy Angle™, and the Companion Angle™. See the General Directions for cutting supplies you'll need to have on hand, and practice the cuts before you plunge into a project. Because you'll be using a sharp rotary cutter, be sure to exercise safety with the blade. Keep the hand holding the tool away from the rotary cutter, and cut gently and smoothly away from the body. It should be pretty effortless to cut. If you have to really push on the cutter, either you're doing it wrong or the blade is too dull or screwed down too tightly.

Cutting Fabric Strips in Preparation

Straighten the edge of the fabric. Using the fabric as it comes off of the bolt, line up the selvages. Align the short end of a 24" ruler on the fold of the fabric. (This will help to prevent a "V" shape in the cut strip.) Trim the edge off evenly.

After you have made this first trim, align the bulk of the fabric toward your dominant hand. Cut the strips from left to right if you are right-handed. Reverse if you are left-handed and cut strips from right to left. After the strips are cut, trim off the selvages before cutting the smaller pieces called for in the patterns. Leave the strips folded, begin cutting from the selvage end. Cut only two layers at a time to maintain the best accuracy. Oftentimes, one more shape can be cut if the folded end is opened.

TRI-RECS™ TOOLS

Use the Tri-Recs™ tools to cut triangles which, when sewn together, form a triangle within a square. The Recs™ tool, used alone, cuts triangles which form a divided rectangle. The proportions of this rectangle are easy to remember: the long edge is simply twice the short edge.

To Cut Tri Triangles

Lay the tool on the strip with the top flat edge at the top of the strip, and a line on the tool aligned with the bottom of the strip. Cut on both sides of the triangle. The width of the strip will be listed in the Fabric & Cutting Guide under "First Cut"; it is always ½" larger than the finished height of the triangle.

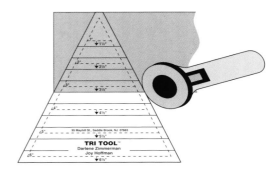

For the second cut, rotate the tool so it is pointing down. Align as before and cut.

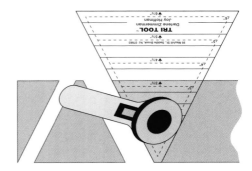

To Cut Recs Triangles

If the Recs triangle is paired with a Tri triangle, use a strip cut to the same width strip as for the Tri pieces. Otherwise, use a strip cut ½" wider than the finished height of the Recs triangle.

Leave the strip folded and you will automatically cut pairs of Recs triangles, one facing left and one facing right. Position the tool with the flat top edge aligned with the top of the strip, and a marked line on the tool aligned with the bottom of the strip. Cut on the angled edge.

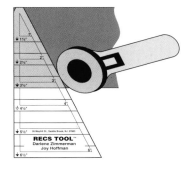

Next, use the rotary cutter to nip off the tiny "magic angle" at the top. Cut accurately: this "magic angle" is your alignment guide when sewing the pieces together.

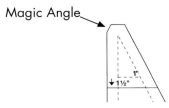

For the second cut, rotate the tool so it is pointing down. Align as before and cut, then trim off the "magic angle."

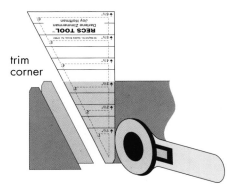

To Combine the Tri and Recs Shapes for a Triangle Within a Square: Lay out the pieces as shown below. Layer the Recs triangle right sides together with the Tri triangle. Notice how the "magic angle" will fit right into the corner and align with the base of the triangle. After the pieces are sewn together and pressed, the seams won't extend into the corner of the newly formed square (the Tri Recs unit), as they do with a triangle square. Instead, they will be offset just a bit, to allow for the seam allowance needed when the Tri Recs unit is sewn into a quilt block. They will be correct once sewn into place in the quilt block.

Divided Rectangles Using Recs Triangles: Carefully layer two strips of fabric together with the right sides of both fabric strips facing up. Now when the Recs triangles are cut, they will all be identical, rather than left and right facing pairs. Check the Cutting Notes, the Fabric & Cutting Guide, and the How-To's to see which kind of Recs you need for that specific project.

Place two Recs triangles right sides together, fitting the "magic angle" into the corner as shown. Once again, the seam will not extend right to the corner of the divided rectangle, but will be just right once the unit is sewn into the quilt. Stitch and press toward the darker fabric.

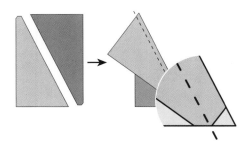

TRI-MATE™

The Tri-Mate™ cuts a triangle with a base that is four times as long as the height. Two Tri-Mate triangles combined with two Tri triangles will make an Hourglass shape (below, left).

A Tri-Mate triangle, combined with a pair of Recs triangles, makes a triangle within a rectangle that resembles half of an hourglass shape, or a long, skinny Flying Goose unit (above, right).

The strip width for Tri-Mate triangles will be ½" larger than the height of the finished triangle.

To cut with the Tri-Mate™, position the tool with the flat top point aligned with the top of the strip, and a marked line on the tool aligned with the bottom of the strip. Since this is a long, thin triangle, take care to keep the bottom edge of the tool aligned with the edge of the fabric strip. Cut on both sides of the tool.

Reposition the tool so that the narrow, angled corners fit into the corner on one side of the base, and trim the point off the fabric to match the tool's corner. This cut will facilitate alignment of pieces (similar to the "magic angle" on the Recs tool). Reposition the tool and trim the corner on the other side of the base in the same way.

Rotate the tool for the next cut so the point of the tool is at the bottom of the strip, and a line on the tool is aligned with the bottom of the strip. Cut again and trim the corners at the base of the triangle as you did before.

Continue in this manner along the strip of fabric.

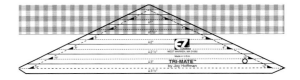

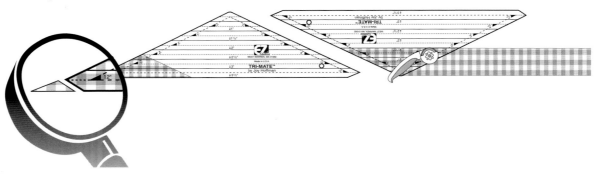

EASY ANGLE™

Use the Easy Angle tool to cut half-square triangles. These triangles have the straight of grain along the short sides of the triangle. To determine the width of the strip you need, simply add ½" to the height of the finished triangle.

The Easy Angle tool comes in two different sizes, 4½" and 6½". You may use either size when Easy Angle triangles are called for in this book.

Line up the bottom edge of the Easy Angle™ on the bottom edge of the fabric strips. Slide the tool to the right until the marked line on the tool that corresponds with the strip width aligns with the edge of the fabric strip. Cut along the diagonal edge with the rotary cutter.

For the next cut, flip the tool up (like turning a page in a book) and line up the top edge of the fabric with the strip size on the tool. The black tip of the tool extends below the bottom of the strip. Cut on the right edge.

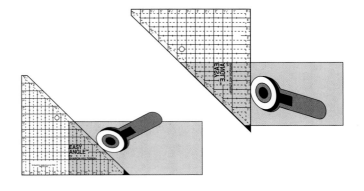

COMPANION ANGLE

Use the Companion Angle to cut quarter-square triangles—triangles with the straight-of-grain along the longest edge. The proportions are simple—the base of the finished triangle is twice the height. To determine the strip width you'll need, simply add ½" to the height of the triangle. Or, if you know the finished base size of the triangle, find that size on the markings along the sides of the tool. The center marking will tell you what size strip to cut.

To cut with Companion Angle, position the tool with the top flat point aligned with the top edge of the strip, and a marked line on the tool aligned with the bottom of the strip. Cut along both sides of the tool.

For the next cut, rotate the tool so the point of the tool is at the bottom of the strip, and a marked line on the tool is aligned with the top of the strip. Cut as before.

Continue in this manner along the strip of fabric.

A common use for this the Companion Angle triangle is the "goose" in a Flying Geese unit, and setting triangles for quilts set on point. Use Easy Angle triangles, cut from strips of the same width, for the background pieces.

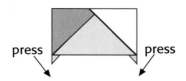

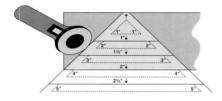

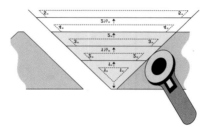

Return to the previous position (turn the page back again) to cut the next triangle.

If you want to cut half-square triangles that will be combined into triangle squares, use this speedy method: Layer two fabric strips right sides together, then cut with Easy Angle. Then, keeping the layered pairs intact, take the cut, half-square triangles to your sewing machine and chain-sew triangle squares, one right after the other.

Continue in this manner along the strip. Chain-sew the triangles on the longest edge. Press toward the darkest fabric and trim "dog-ears."

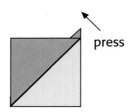

See page 80 for information on purchasing these tools.

71

TRIANGLE TABLE

This reference guide tells you how many triangles of a certain type and height can be cut from a 42" wide strip of fabric. Refer to this information to determine how much more (or less) fabric may be needed if you decide to make your quilt in a different size, whether by using a smaller or larger block or unit, or by decreasing or increasing the number of repeats in the quilt assembly. You can also use this table to calculate your yardage needs for a new and original design which features these shapes.

The Tri-Mate™ and Companion Angle™ tools also indicate finished sizes for the base of the triangle you will cut. These numbers appear along both sides of each tool. If you know the base of the triangle you need but not the height, look on the center of the tool between the base measurements. This measurement (with an arrow pointing to the solid line which you'll align with the edge of the strip) indicates the finished height of the triangle and width of the fabric strip required.

Height of Finished Triangle	Width of Fabric Strip	Easy Angle Triangles	Companion Angle Triangles	Tri Triangles	Recs Triangles	Tri-Mate Triangles
½"	1"	50	34			
¾"	1¼"	42	27			14
1"	1½"	38	23	38	52	11
1¼"	1¾"	32	20			9
1½"	2"	30	17	31	44	8
1¾"	2¼"	28	16			8
2"	2½"	26	13	25	40	8
2¼"	2¾"	24	13			6
2½"	3"	22	12	21	34	5
2¾"	3¼"	20	10			5
3"	3½"	20	9	19	32	4
3¼"	3¾"	18	9			
3½"	4"	18	8	17	28	
3¾"	4¼"	16	7			
4"	4½"	16	7	15	24	
4¼"	4¾"	14	7			
4½"	5"	14	7	13	24	
4¾"	5¼"	14	7			
5"	5½"	12	5	12	22	
5¼"	5¾"	12	5			
5½"	6"	12		11	22	
5¾"	6¼"	12				
6"	6½"	12		10	20	

GENERAL DIRECTIONS FOR QUILTMAKING

For quiltmaking as in all endeavors, preparation and planning will make everything go more smoothly and you'll end up enjoying the process a lot more. When you are inspired to make one of the designs in this book, get a sense for the entire project first. Read through all the directions for that project, through the General Directions here, and also through the Tool Tutorial for instructions and tips on the use of the key tools.

Choosing Fabrics

Don't be intimidated by color when choosing fabrics. Trust your instincts. You know what colors you or the recipient of your quilt favor, what colors you like in your home or have seen in the homes your gift quilt will be beautifying.

CONTRASTING COLORS AND VALUES

Be sure to keep a mix of light, medium and dark values for contrast and interest. You may enjoy shades of beige and cream in your decorating scheme, but a quilt made only in those colors could be as bland as oatmeal! Put some dark brown sugar and a few "raisins" into the mixture and you will be delighted with the results this contrast of values can add.

Here's another method of choosing colors that is stress-free, even for color-challenged quilters: Pick a multicolor print that you really love. Select bolts of fabric that duplicate the colors in this print, and use them as the color palette for the quilt. The original fabric may or may not be used in the quilt, but because you took the colors directly from a favorite print, the colors chosen for the quilt will be as delightful to your eye as the original fabric.

How to judge if you have enough color contrast? Step back at least 10 feet from your selections and squint. Do all the colors bleed together or do you have some accents that stand out?

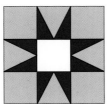

USE TEXTURES

If you look closely at the photographs in this book, you'll notice that there are very few quilts that feature solid colored fabrics. With the exception of hand-dyed fabrics in gradations, most of the fabrics that may read as solids are actually prints. These "solid substitutes"—mottled, speckled, or tone-on-tone prints are usually more interesting than true solids, and they give more depth and visual texture to the quilt.

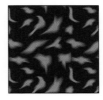 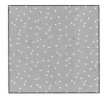 

It's also important to consider the scale of the printed fabrics. All tiny or "nothing" prints can be boring, while a quilt entirely made up of large busy prints will overwhelm the design. Use a mix of solid substitutes, small or quiet prints, medium-scale prints, and large or busy prints, and your finished quilt will be much more successful.

QUALITY & CARE

No matter what colors or types of prints you decide on, purchase the best quality, 100% cotton fabric available. The extra investment will be rewarded in the finished appearance of the quilt and in the ease of handling. Wash your fabrics in warm water with gentle soap or detergent, to check for colorfastness and to pre-shrink the fabrics.

Pressing the fabric using spray starch will add extra body, making the fabric pieces easier to cut and handle, and less likely to stretch out of shape when you're working with them—especially those bias edges. Once the quilt is completed, it's best to rinse out the starch, as well as any marks made for quilting.

Using the Fabric & Cutting Guide

The Fabric & Cutting Guide will tell you how much fabric you need for each project. Be sure to read the Cutting Notes that precede the chart, so you know what to cut first, and how to layer fabrics for speed and convenience.

Two important notes about borders, which you'll need to know from the very beginning:

● The Fabric & Cutting Guide provides the measurements for cutting plain (unpieced) borders strips. These dimensions represent the mathematical ideal—in other words, this is the length they would be if your cutting, piecing, and pressing is absolutely precise, which of course is never the case. If you cut the borders early in the quiltmaking process, it is essential that you cut these pieces extra long, so that you don't end up with pieces that are too short when you're ready to join them to the quilt center. You may have your own system, but if not, add 2" to the given length for smaller quilts, and add 4" for the larger quilts, just for insurance. This extra length will get trimmed off as the assembly is completed.

● Some of the patterns in this book call for plain (unpieced) borders cut lengthwise (parallel to the selvage), so that you will not have seams in the borders. When this is the case, you need to cut these pieces first, then use the remaining fabric to cut shorter strips from which to cut the smaller pieces. Save a bit of time by simply adding the widths of the borders to be cut and cutting one large piece to be used as borders. For example: if four 3" borders are needed—add them all together and just cut one 12" piece. Set it aside and cut it into the exact borders when needed.

Note: Some quilters prefer to cut their borders along the width, and piece their borders. They do this to save fabric, or because they like to hold off making their border fabric decisions until after the quilt center is completed.

● If you are pre-cutting spacer borders—those versatile plain borders that bridge the distance between pieced borders and the quilt center, you'll need to add insurance to the width as well as the length, to allow for the inevitable departures from that mathematical ideal and ensure a perfect fit during the assembly process.

For more tips on adding borders, see page 76.

ELEMENT/FABRIC

Look at the first vertical column of a Fabric & Cutting Guide. The part of the quilt design or element—border strip, patch, background, or binding—is provided, as well as the color or pattern of the fabric as it's used in the photographed quilt. This is meant to make it easy for you to substitute your own personal choices for colors and patterns. So, if you want to make the Big & Little Fishies twin-size quilt as it's shown on page 23 and 27, you'll have a shopping list to take to the quilt store, and you'll know that you need 7 yards of blue fabric for the watery background. While that fabric is a mottled blue in the quilt that's photographed, there's nothing to stop you from using a celadon green, a dark turquoise, or any color you want for the water in your quilt.

YARDAGES

In the second column of the Fabric & Cutting Guide, the yardage amount is provided, but only the first time each fabric is listed. For example, if there are House Front patches in the blocks shown in the quilt as red, it will be designated as House Front/red in the chart, the column next to that may contain the amount 1½" yards (far more than is needed for just the patches). However, the binding that (as shown) repeats the same fabric does not give any yardage amount. This is because you will be using the same yardage goods for that part of the quilt. Of course, if you think you will want to cut the binding from another fabric, you'll need less red fabric. On the other hand, if you want the borders—in addition to the House Front and the binding— to be red, you'll need to purchase more red fabric. The numbers in the third column will give you a good idea as to how much more or less fabric you will need to make the changes.

FIRST & SECOND CUTS

The third column of the Fabric & Cutting Guide is the first cut: usually the strips you will rotary cut along the width of the fabric (unless you are cutting borders along the length). The last column is the second cut: these are either the subcuts, or squares and rectangles that you'll cut using your acrylic rulers, or the triangles you'll cut from these strips, using the key tools: the Tri-Recs™, Tri-Mate™, Easy Angle™, and Companion Angle™ tools. Rember to consult the Tool Tutorial on pages 68-71 for cutting these shapes accurately.

Cutting

SUPPLIES

For making the pieced designs in this book, success begins at the cutting table. Here are some basic supplies you'll want to have on hand:

- A long, rectangular acrylic ruler for cutting strips. The Super Quickline Ruler, Easy Rule, and Easy Rule Jr. are good choices.

- A mat with a smooth surface. Replace any mat that is nicked and grooved from many, many cuts.

- A rotary cutter. Treat yourself to a new, sharp blade, to make cutting effortless.

KEY TOOLS

The specific cutting tools for these projects will be listed at the beginning of the set of directions for the particular design you want to make. Go over the directions for the tool(s) you need in the Tool Tutorial on pages 68-71. Practice cutting and sewing a few units, using scraps of the same quality fabrics you will be using for your project, until you become comfortable working with the tools.

STEPS TO CUTTING SUCCESS

- Don't cut in the shadows. Be sure there is comfortable natural light or suitable artificial light.

- Straighten the edge of the fabric. Using the fabric as it comes off of the bolt, line up the selvages. Align the short end of a 24" ruler on the fold of the fabric. (This will help to prevent a "V" shape in the cut strip.) Trim the edge off evenly.

- After you have made this first trim, align the bulk of the fabric toward your dominant hand. Cut the strips from left to right if you are right-handed. Reverse if you are left-handed and cut strips from right to left.

- Cut only two layers of fabric at one time to maintain accuracy.

- Be sure to use the correct tool to cut the pieces. Easy Angle and Companion Angle both cut right triangles, but the shapes and sizes are not interchangeable.

- Cut enough pieces to make one block or unit to test for cutting/sewing accuracy and the placement and choice of fabrics. Step back and view the sample block from a distance. Take the time to try different arrangements of fabrics and colors until you like the look of the block.

- Keep the pieces identified as they are cut. To do this, try this system: put patches of the same type on an inexpensive paper plate, and label the plate with the design element, or part of the quilt design, for which those pieces will be used. Stack the plates as needed and carry them from your cutting table to the sewing machine.

Piecing

EQUIPMENT

Be sure your sewing machine is in good working order. Now is the time to clean out the "fuzzies"—that lint along the feed dogs and bobbin case. Add a drop of oil, if appropriate for your machine, and a sharp, new needle—70/10 is a good size for piecing. Use a standard weight sewing thread (40 or 50)— cotton, poly, or a cotton-covered polyester. If you have lots of different colors in your project, a neutral beige or gray should blend with all your fabrics.

THE PERFECT SEAM

Sewing an exact ¼" seam is essential. Mark the quarter inch on your sewing machine with a seam guide as follows: Set the needle down gently on the ¼" mark of an acrylic ruler. Lower the presser foot. Place a strip of masking tape on your machine bed, along the edge of the ruler, forming a stitching guide that is exactly ¼" from the needle. Don't cover the feed dogs with the tape.

Try this test for an accurate ¼" seam allowance: Sew together three 1½" × 3½" rectangles to form a square. It should be a 3½" square (raw edge to raw edge) after the seams are sewn. If it's not, adjust your seam allowance as well as your pressing technique until the sample block does measure 3½".

Pin to line up seams and match points, but pull out pins just before your machine needle comes to them—never sew over pins.

Pressing

Good pressing is important for crisp, precise pieced quilts. Set the seam as it's sewn, then use the tip of the iron to unfold the top layer and press the seam allowances to one side. If the darker-fabric patch is on top, the seam allowances will naturally fall toward the darker fabric.

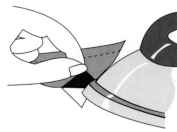

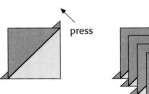

press

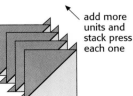

add more units and stack press each one

Be sure to press your seam allowances before you cross them with another seam. Press them in the direction indicated by the little arrows in the diagrams, or as directed in the How-To's. If no directions or pressing arrows are provided, use these rules of thumb:

● Press seam allowances towards the darker fabric, to avoid shadow through.

● Press seam allowances towards the edges that have the fewest number of seams, to lessen bulk.

● For perfect points where two pieced units are being joined, press the seam allowances in opposing directions, so they will butt up against each other.

● If there are more than two seams coming together at an intersection, press the seam allowances open, to better distribute the bulk of so many layers.

Whenever a section or the entire quilt top is completed, press thoroughly using an up and down motion (rather than ironing with a back and forth motion). Using steam for the final pressing will help to achieve a flat, straight block. Don't handle fabric that is damp and hot from steam—it's too easy to stretch and distort the quilt block. Wait until the fabric is cool and dry before moving it from the ironing board.

Adding Borders

AUDITIONING FABRICS

Border suggestions have been made for all the projects in this book, but your quilt may be better complimented by a different choice of fabric. Place the borders around the completed quilt center, and step back to assess how well the border frames, unifies, and balances the design. If you're not entirely satisfied, audition some other fabrics for the borders, and see if a stronger candidate emerges.

TRIMMING AND STITCHING THE BORDERS

If you wisely gave yourself some extra insurance in the length of the plain (unpieced) border strips you pre-cut, now is the time to trim them to size. Here is a simple method to determine the correct sizes for your completed quilt center. The edges of the quilt center may have stretched with handling, so measure the quilt top vertically through the middle, rather than along the raw edges. (One easy way to determine the border lengths is to cut border strips longer than needed for the top and bottom, and use each strip as a "ruler.") Adding an inch or two for

insurance, cut two border strips to that same measurement. Pin to the quilt, then sew to the top and bottom of the quilt. Press the seam allowances toward the borders, then trim off the excess fabric from the border strips.

Measure the quilt top vertically through the center, including the borders just added. (Use a border strip to do your measuring as before, if you prefer.) Cut two border strips to that length plus a bit extra for insurance. Pin to the quilt, then sew to the sides of the quilt. Press the seam allowances toward the borders, then trim off the excess fabric from the border strips.

Generally, border strips are joined to the top and bottom of the quilt, then to the sides, as explained above. However, there are times when, in the interest of saving fabric or to avoid piecing a border, the side border strips are joined first.

BORDERS CUT ALONG THE LENGTH OF THE FABRIC

To repeat information emphasized on page 74, some of the Fabric & Cutting Guides and How-To's in this book call for borders cut lengthwise (parallel to the selvage) to avoid seams in the borders. Lengthwise borders are also very stable as the lengthwise grain has the least amount of stretch, and this helps prevent wavy borders.

SPACER BORDERS

Pieced borders can add a wonderful frame to a quilt. If the pieced borders are made up of precise units, a plain border—or spacer border—serves to bridge the distance between the quilt center and the pieced border, and ensures that the pieced border will fit perfectly. The designs in this book that have pieced borders also have cornerstones—a plain or pieced square at the corner of the pieced border. To keep things simple, wait to sew that cornerstone onto the pieced border until after the spacer borders have been added.

Whether you're cutting spacer borders after the quilt center and pieced borders are completed, or trimming down the ones you generously cut early on, you need to calculate the exact widths of those spacer borders. Directions are as follows and will give you borders that are sized just right for your quilt rather than the mathematical ideal size given in the pattern (which may be very close):

SPACER BORDERS FOR THE SIDES OF THE QUILT

1. Measure across the quilt center from side to side—raw edge to raw edge. Subtract ½" from this number, to determine the finished width of the quilt center. (As an example, if the quilt center measures 58" across, the finished size is 57½".)

2. Measure along the length of the pieced border that will be sewn to the top or bottom of the quilt—from raw edge to raw edge. Subtract ½" from this number as well to determine its finished size. (If the pieced border measures 62½", the finished size is 62".)

3. Subtract the finished quilt center measurement from the finished pieced border measurement. (In our example, that would be: 62" – 57½" = 4½".)

4. Divide this number by 2, to provide an equal amount of space at both sides of the quilt (4½ ÷ 2 = 2¼"). You now have the finished width for each of two spacer borders needed. Add ½" to this number for the seam allowances (2¼" + ½" = 2¾") to determine the width to cut these spacer borders. For the length, match the dimensions of the quilt center. Cut the two spacer borders to these measurements. Sew these borders in place, and press the seam allowances toward the borders.

SPACER BORDERS FOR THE TOP AND BOTTOM OF THE QUILT

5. Measure the quilt center from top to bottom—raw edge to raw edge. Subtract ½" to get the finished size. (In our example, 72½" – ½" = 72".)

6. Measure the length of the pieced borders (without cornerstones) that will go on the sides of the quilt—raw edge to raw edge. Subtract ½" to get the finished size. (In our example: 76" – ½" = 75½".)

7. Subtract the finished quilt center measurement from the finished pieced border measurement (75½" – 72" = 3½").

8. Divide this number by 2, to provide an equal amount of space at both the top and bottom of the quilt (3½" ÷ 2 = 1¾"). You now have the finished width for the spacer borders needed for the top and bottom of the quilt. Add ½" for the seam allowances (1¾" + ½" = 2¼"). This is the width to cut the spacer borders to be sewn to the top and bottom of the quilt center. For the length, measure across the quilt top from raw edge to raw edge (the quilt center plus the spacer borders along the sides). Cut space borders to these measurements, and sew them to the top and bottom of the quilt top. Press the seam allowances toward the borders.

ADD THE PIECED BORDERS

Stitch pieced borders to two opposite sides of the quilt top; press the seam allowances toward the spacer border. Stitch the cornerstones to the ends of the remaining pieced borders, and press toward the cornerstones. Pin the pieced borders to the spacer borders, taking care to match the seam of the cornerstone with the seam between the pieced border and the spacer border. Stitch in place, and press the seam allowances toward the spacer borders.

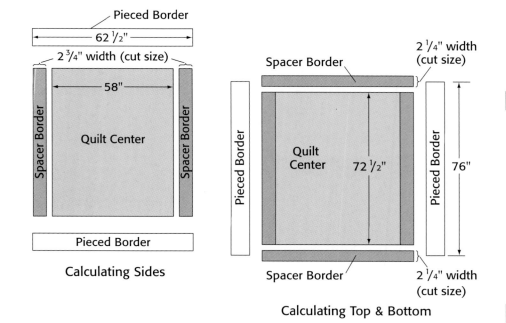

Calculating Sides

Calculating Top & Bottom

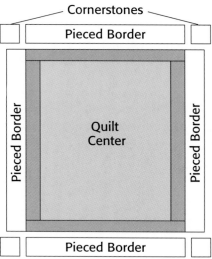

Adding Pieced Borders

Finishing the Quilt

BACKING

When the quilt top is completed, you will need a quilt backing that is at least 4" larger than the top, or 2" extra along each edge. For the larger quilts, piece fabric to obtain the necessary dimensions, or purchase extra-wide fabric specially created for quilt backings.

BATTING

Cut batting to the same size as the backing. As for the type of batting, choose it to suit the style quilt you have made, as well as the desired finished appearance. Be sure to read the labels to avoid any surprises. A very thin batt, either cotton or polyester, is best for wall-hangings, tablerunners, and tablecloths. Projects which you intend to hand quilt will be easiest to stitch with a low loft batt. The very puffiest batts should be reserved for tied comforters.

Cotton batting tends to shrink, sometimes a considerable amount. Test-wash a quilted sample square in the washer so you can note the result and the actual amount of shrinkage. Shrinkage will give an antique, puckered look to a quilt, which may be just the look you want. Cotton batts can sometimes be harder to stitch through when hand-quilting; try quilting a small test sample first to see if you will be able to work comfortably. Cotton batting is nice to use for machine quilting, as the quilt layers will not shift as readily as with a polyester batt.

Polyester batts come in a range of lofts from quite thin to very thick. A finished quilt made with a polyester batt is generally lighter in weight and fluffier than it would be had it contained a cotton batt. It is also quite shrink-resistant, so the finished quilt will not change significantly in size after washing. Polyester batts are available in a charcoal gray color as well as white; consider a gray batt for any dark-colored quilt where bearding—little bits of batting fibers coming through the quilt—could be a problem.

QUILTING

The type and style of quilting used to finish the quilt are very individual choices, based on your preferences for hand vs. machine quilting, and for the quilting designs that appeal to you, and also for the amount of time available to you. We offer a suggested design for quilting each project, but these are simply that: suggestions. Consider all sorts of designs or branch out with an original design.

Always test your marking tool on some fabric scraps from your project to be sure that the marks can be easily removed when the quilting is completed. Different dyes and finishes on the fabric may react differently than expected to a familiar marking pencil or chalk. Always mark as lightly as possible to facilitate easy removal. If you are using a wash-out marker (typically blue) or a pencil type of marking tool, mark the quilt top before the layering and basting is done. If you prefer to use a chalk pencil or chalk wheel to mark, work in one section at a time on the layered, basted quilt, as the chalk tends to brush off quickly.

Layering and Basting

Before basting, press the backing and quilt top carefully. Watch for and remove any stray threads which may shadow through. Lay out the backing fabric right side down on the floor or other flat surface large enough to accommodate it. Tape the edges down with masking tape every 8" to 12". Layer the batting on top, smoothing out wrinkles. Place the quilt top right sides up on top of the other two layers, making sure you have extra batting and backing extending beyond the quilt top on all four sides.

Baste the three layers together with large stitches sewn in a 4" grid, or safety pins placed approximately every 4". Turn the extra backing up over the raw edges of the quilt sandwich and baste in place—this will help keep the edges from fraying as the quilting is done.

Binding

To prepare for the binding, hand-baste a scant ¼" from the edge of the quilt top through all the layers. This will prevent the layers from shifting while the binding is added.

If your quilt is a wall hanging, create a simple hanging sleeve at this stage and pin to the back, so that the edges on one long side will be encased in the binding along the top edge.

There are lots of methods for binding quilts, and the How-To's in this book suggest a particular type of binding for each quilt project. However, be guided by your preferences, as well as the way you want a directional fabric to appear. Generally speaking, a single-fold, straight-of-grain binding is ideal for a small wall hanging, where a double fold binding would be too bulky. Single-fold bias binding is flexible, making it the best choice for curves. Double-fold, straight-of-grain binding gives a heavier finish that is appropriate for larger quilts. However, for quilts that will see heavy use, a binding with only one thread running along the fold line would fray easily. In such instances, use a double-fold, bias binding, the strongest and most durable type.

Cutting, Joining, and Pressing the Strips

Cut single fold binding strips 1¼" wide. Cut double-fold binding strips 2¼" wide.

To cut bindings along the straight-of-grain, cut enough strips along the width of the fabric until you have enough, in total, to go around the entire quilt, plus 12"–18" extra to allow for joins and turning corners. To cut bindings along the bias, align the 45 degree mark on your longest ruler with the selvage of the fabric. Cut along the edge of the ruler. Move the ruler over 2¼" (or the width of your binding) and cut another strip in the same way. Continue in this manner across the width of the fabric.

Join the strips, whether straight-or-grain or bias, with diagonal seams pressed open, until the total length is at least 12" longer than the distance all around the quilt.

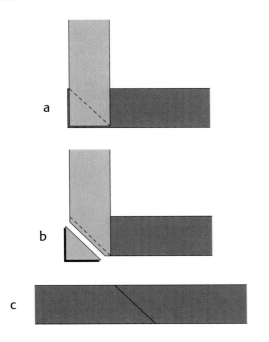

For single-fold bindings, press one long edge a scant ¼" to the wrong side; machine stitch the binding to the quilt along the opposite long edge. For double-fold bindings, fold the binding in half lengthwise with the wrong side in; press.

To Attach Binding:

Begin at the bottom of the quilt at least 6" away from a corner, and leave a 6" tail (approximately). Match the raw edges of the binding to the raw edge of the quilt top. Use a walking foot (also called an even feed foot) to help keep the layers of the quilt from shifting while the binding is being sewn on the quilt. Stitch the binding to the quilt leaving ¼" seam allowances.

For stitching along curved edges such as scallops, handle the single-fold bias strips gently so they don't stretch out of shape. Ease the binding around the curves, stopping when you get to the bottom of the "V" in a scallop. Put the needle down, lift the presser foot, and pivot the quilt and the binding around the needle. Align the quilt and binding to stitch out of the "V." Lower the presser foot and stitch out of the "V."

Miter the corners using the following steps. Stop stitching ¼" away from the corner and backstitch. Remove the quilt from under the presser foot. Turn the quilt so the next side is aligned to sew. Pull the binding straight up away from the quilt, then back down, aligned with the next edge to be sewn. There should be a fold at the top edge of the quilt. Start sewing at the edge, catching the fold in the seam. Miter each corner in this way.

To finish the binding, trim the ends diagonally so they overlap, and fold under the overlapping end as shown below. Finish sewing the binding to the quilt.

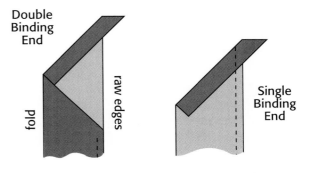

Trim off excess batting and backing, leaving enough seam allowance and batting to "fill" the binding. Fold the binding to the back of the quilt so it covers the stitching lines, and pin in place. Working by hand with a needle and thread that matches the binding, slipstitch the foldline of the binding to the backing.

A Quilt Label

It's a wonderful idea to create a label for every quilt you make. This is a future heirloom, so don't neglect this part of quiltmaking! Pertinent information (name of the quilt, who made it, when, where, and for whom it was intended) may be written on a purchased label, using a Pigma pen for permanent writing on fabric. As a unique alternative, create a label from a miniature block or leftover units from the quilt top. Turn the edges under, and stitch the label to the backing. Perhaps you'll want to add a bit of surface quilting—taking hand-quilting stitches through the label and batting, but not through to the front of the quilt. This will attach the label to the quilt back securely, and also add texture and interest.

Quilts To Come Home To is the third book Joy Hoffman and Darlene Zimmerman have coauthored, after *The Quilter's Kitchen* and *Calming the Storm.* They have also collaborated in developing the popular Tri-Recs™ tools. Individually, each has developed other quilting tools for EZ Quilting by Wrights, and each is a prolific quilt designer, and a sought-after quilt teacher. Their homes are in rural southwestern Minnesota, about a half hour drive apart.

Joy is the creator of the Tri-Mate™ tool, as well as the Sliding Stencil™, a group of adjustable quilting stencils. She has written quilt patterns and articles for *American Patchwork and Quilting, McCall's Quilting,* and *Quick and Easy Quilts.* Joy is the mother of one high school student and two college students, and is also involved in the running of her husband's certified organic grain and poultry farm. She muses, "If those chickens could just learn to lay eggs directly in the cartons, think of the time that would be available for quiltmaking!"

Darlene is the inventor of the Companion Angle™ and the Easy Scallop™. She is a frequent contributor to *American Patchwork and Quilting* magazine, *McCalls' Vintage Quilts* and *Quiltmaker* magazine. She designs the *Granny's Apron Prints* line of fabric and others for Chanteclaire Fabrics, based on her collection of vintage fabric. Darlene lives in a small town with her husband and the youngest of their four children; the eldest three have left the nest. One daughter was married last summer, another is to be married this summer, and all the children are rivals for Mom's quilts—if not her attentions.

Purchasing Information

The Tri-Recs™, Tri-Mate™, Easy Angle™, and Companion Angle™ tools, as well as the Sliding Stencil™, and Easy Scallop™ are produced by EZ Quilting by Wrights. Look for these tools and other books by Darlene Zimmerman and Joy Hoffman wherever quilting supplies are sold, or contact:

EZ Quilting by Wrights
P.O. Box 398
West Warren, MA 01092-0398
Telephone: (800)628-9362
Web site: www.wrights.com
or www.ezquilt.com